STANDING IN GOD'S HOLY FIRE

TRADITIONS OF CHRISTIAN SPIRITUALITY SERIES

STANDING IN GOD'S HOLY FIRE

The Byzantine Tradition

JOHN ANTHONY McGUCKIN

SERIES EDITOR:
Philip Sheldrake

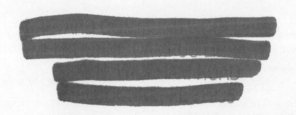

ORBIS **BOOKS**
Maryknoll, New York 10545

Founded in 1970, Orbis Books endeavors to publish works that enlighten the mind, nourish the spirit, and challenge the conscience. The publishing arm of the Maryknoll Fathers & Brothers, Orbis seeks to explore the global dimensions of the Christian faith and mission, to invite dialogue with diverse cultures and religious traditions, and to serve the cause of reconciliation and peace. The books published reflect the views of their authors and do not represent the official position of the Maryknoll Society. To learn more about Maryknoll and Orbis Books, please visit our website at www.maryknoll.org.

First published in Great Britain in 2001 by
Darton, Longman and Todd Ltd
1 Spencer Court
140–142 Wandsworth High Street
London SW18 4JJ
Great Britain

Published in the USA in 2001 by
Orbis Books
P.O. Box 308
Maryknoll, New York 10545–0308
U.S.A.

ISBN 1–57075–382–2

Printed and bound in Great Britain.

Library of Congress Cataloging-in-Publication Data

McGuckin, John Anthony.
   Standing in God's holy fire: the Byzantine spiritual tradition / by J. A. McGuckin.
       p.   cm.—(Traditions of Christian spirituality series)
   Includes bibliographical references.
   ISBN 1–57075–382–2 (pbk.)
   1. Spirituality—Orthodox Eastern Church.   I. Title.   II. Traditions of Christian spirituality.
BX382.M34   2001
281′.5—dc21
                                                                        2001036538

For Archbishop Serafim Joanta
who lives out and teaches all these things

CONTENTS

CONTENTS

PREFACE TO THE SERIES

Nowadays, in the western world, there is a widespread hunger for spirituality in all its forms. This is not confined to traditional religious people let alone to regular churchgoers. The desire for resources to sustain the spiritual quest has led many people to seek wisdom in unfamiliar places. Some have turned to cultures other than their own. The fascination with Native American or Aboriginal Australian spiritualities is a case in point. Other people have been attracted by the religions of India and Tibet or the Jewish Kabbalah and Sufi mysticism. One problem is that, in comparison to other religions, Christianity is not always associated in people's minds with 'spirituality'. The exceptions are a few figures from the past who have achieved almost cult status such as Hildegard of Bingen or Meister Eckhart. This is a great pity, for Christianity East and West over two thousand years has given birth to an immense range of spiritual wisdom. Many traditions continue to be active today. Others that were forgotten are being rediscovered and reinterpreted.

It is a long time since an extended series of introductions to Christian spiritual traditions has been available in English. Given the present climate, it is an opportune moment for a new series which will help more people to be aware of the great spiritual riches available within the Christian tradition.

The overall purpose of the series is to make selected spiritual traditions available to a contemporary readership. The books seek to provide accurate and balanced historical and thematic treatments of their subjects. The authors are also conscious of the need to make connections with contemporary experience

and values without being artificial or reducing a tradition to
one dimension. The authors are well versed in reliable scholarship about the traditions they describe. However, their
intention is that the books should be fresh in style and accessible to the general reader.

One problem that such a series inevitably faces is the word
'spirituality'. For example, it is increasingly used beyond
religious circles and does not necessarily imply a faith tradition. Again, it could mean substantially different things for
a Christian and a Buddhist. Within Christianity itself, the
word in its modern sense is relatively recent. The reality that
it stands for differs subtly in the different contexts of time and
place. Historically, 'spirituality' covers a breadth of human
experience and a wide range of values and practices.

No single definition of 'spirituality' has been imposed on the
authors in this series. Yet, despite the breadth of the series
there is a sense of a common core in the writers themselves
and in the traditions they describe. All Christian spiritual
traditions have their source in three things. First, while
drawing on ordinary experience and even religious insights
from elsewhere, Christian spiritualities are rooted in the Scriptures and particularly in the Gospels. Second, spiritual
traditions are not derived from abstract theory but from
attempts to live out gospel values in a positive yet critical
way within specific historical and cultural contexts. Third, the
experiences and insights of individuals and groups are not
isolated but are related to the wider Christian tradition of
beliefs, practices and community life. From a Christian perspective, spirituality is not just concerned with prayer or even
with narrowly religious activities. It concerns the whole of
human life, viewed in terms of a conscious relationship with
God, in Jesus Christ, through the indwelling of the Holy Spirit
and within a community of believers.

The series as a whole includes traditions that probably
would not have appeared twenty years ago. The authors themselves have been encouraged to challenge, where appropriate,
inaccurate assumptions about their particular tradition. While

conscious of their own biases, authors have none the less sought to correct the imbalances of the past. Previous understandings of what is mainstream or 'orthodox' sometimes need to be questioned. People or practices that became marginal demand to be re-examined. Studies of spirituality in the past frequently underestimated or ignored the role of women. Sometimes the treatments of spiritual traditions were culturally one-sided because they were written from an uncritical Western European or North Atlantic perspective.

However, any series is necessarily selective. It cannot hope to do full justice to the extraordinary variety of Christian spiritual traditions. The principles of selection are inevitably open to question. I hope that an appropriate balance has been maintained between a sense of the likely readership on the one hand and the dangers of narrowness on the other. In the end, choices had to be made and the result is inevitably weighted in favour of traditions that have achieved 'classic' status or which seem to capture the contemporary imagination. Within these limits, I trust that the series will offer a reasonably balanced account of what the Christian spiritual tradition has to offer.

As editor of the series I would like to thank all the authors who agreed to contribute and for the stimulating conversations and correspondence that sometimes resulted. I am especially grateful for the high quality of their work which made my task so much easier. Editing such a series is a complex undertaking. I have worked closely throughout with the editorial team of Darton, Longman and Todd and Robert Ellsberg of Orbis Books. I am immensely grateful to them for their friendly support and judicious advice. Without them this series would never have come together.

PHILIP SHELDRAKE
Sarum College, Salisbury

1. PRELUDE:
BYZANTIUM – A SHORT HISTORY

A FORGOTTEN GLORY

Byzantium.[1] What an image of exotic beauty and strangeness
it connotes. A lost empire with all the allure and mystery of
that idea; fabulous in its wealth and in its artistic and literary
cultures; nurturing a religious spirit that stamped its bread
in the market places and the coins in its citizens' hands, with
images of Christ and the Virgin, one that founded monasteries
and holy places many of which endure to this day as cradles
of Christian pilgrimage.[2] It was the empire of the Romans
brought to submission in Christ; an imperial culture that tried
to synthesise (not always successfully, but certainly with high
seriousness) the spirit of the gospel and the demands of
forming and governing vast and disparate geographical territories. Its sphere of influence stretched from the mountains of
Iran to the highlands of Ethiopia, from the deserts of Arabia
to the forests of England or Russia, from the wheatfields of
North Africa to the coastal cities of Romania and the Black
Sea, from the teeming streets of Alexandria to the villages of
Sicily, Calabria and Yugoslavia. Byzantium: the progenitor
of the very ideas of Christian civilisation and Christian international culture. A city, an imperial capital, a central eye in
the vortex that was the swirl of the chief trade routes of the
ancient world. Its gold coinage was the legendary standard of
the ancient economy. It was poised in the strategic axis of the
old world, with the finest port of antiquity commanding the
spice routes from India, the silk road from China and the
Orient, the fur trade down the river Dnieper from the snowy

cities of Old Rus. It was always the envy of the West, which regarded its glorious cities and systems of government with wonder and emulated them throughout its own cultural history. Balanced at the pivotal point of the ancient Mediterranean world it exercised its influence extensively, not least in the service of the gospel by the missionary impact it had before Islam later cut back and overwhelmed much of its achievement. Even after the loss of the Christian civilisations it once formed in the Orient, and with its own final collapse before the Crescent at the time of the Renaissance, it still lives on in Christian traditions as varied and significant as contemporary patterns of Celtic, Russian, Greek, and African Christian experience. Through its luminously beautiful iconic art, and the writings of its great saints and mystics, it is exercising again in this present time a formative influence on Christian spirituality; and this only rightly, for in its complex theological heritage it laid the foundations of the very substructure of 'catholicity' for all the Churches of East and West.

Yet the Roman Empire of the eastern Christians also conjures up a prejudicial sense too. The modern adjective 'Byzantine' derived from the name of the capital city was often used as a prejudicial convention to signify something exotic and decadently 'oriental'. The English historian Gibbon, in his *History of the Decline and Fall of the Roman Empire*, was largely responsible for making the word almost a synonym for political and moral duplicity. Since his time, more balanced and serious research on the nature of the Greek Christian world has established the study of the Christianity east of Italy as a fundamental part of the search for a defining sense of the Church's identity.[3] The days, not too long ago, when Byzantine architectural remains found on ancient archaeological sites would simply be shovelled away into oblivion in an attempt to establish the real 'classical' civilisation, have rightly begun to pass and yet the Byzantine Christian world continues to suffer neglect: for two main reasons. The first is the ascendancy of western forms of Christianity in the period from the late Middle Ages onwards. The old centres of the Christian

world, with Rome and the Mediterranean coast being their
most westward extensions in antiquity, have long been left
behind as the new epicentre progressively shifted westwards
and northwards, until the axis is probably now in the southern
states of North America. The constant movement, understood
historically, has been not least because of pressure of military
force from the East. That unrelenting pressure of westward-
moving conquests spelled out the political doom for the ancient
Christian heartlands, the cities and political systems in which
the Church of the New Testament and patristic ages was
rooted. As Byzantium, encompassed by Islamic military might,
fell into a slow decline and into its last twilight, so too did the
West enter into its period of great awakening, militarily and
culturally. The records of church history and canons of ecclesiastical judgement that were established then, approached
Byzantium and its religious culture in decidedly biased apologetic ways: it was largely written off as a schismatic Church
with odd traditions that cried out for western 'reforms'. Traditional curricula of western theological schools (and it still
applies abundantly even into the twenty-first-century univer-
sity departments of theology and religion) felt they could
operate perfectly well with little, if any, mention of the entire
eastern Christian experience; and this, even though all the
formative Christian arguments, creeds, liturgies, and practices
were born and developed in a Greek world. So much so that
even the sayings of the Founder were recorded not in their
original language but in Greek translation in the Gospels, and
even the liturgy of the Church of Rome was celebrated, for its
earliest centuries, in the Greek language of the Roman faithful
there.

The western schools traditionally taught, and so it was
imprinted on the general consciousness even into the late
modern age, that the Roman Empire 'fell' sometime in the
early fifth century. It still comes as a surprise to most graduate
students of history to discover that the last of the Roman
emperors, Constantine XI, actually fell in battle defending
the Christian capital in 1453, at the St Romanos Gate of

Constantinople.[4] Byzantium endured as an unbroken
Christian experience from the time the Empire was evangel-
ised in the fourth century until the extinguishing of Christian
liberty in the eastern world in the fifteenth.

The old neglect of eastern church history is slowly being
replaced by a contemporary environment that welcomes more
universalist and inclusive readings of the evidence. The
appearance of this volume among the traditions of Christian
spirituality is a sign of that movement, and it can thus serve
a significant ecumenical purpose. A wider understanding of
Christian origins would go a long way to explaining to western
Christians the nature and condition of the whole shape of
Byzantine and oriental Christianity. The Orthodox Churches
of eastern Europe finally had the last stone taken off their
necks only as recently as the late eighties of the twentieth
century, and others, particularly the Copts of Egypt, or the
Syrian Orthodox, still wait to experience a happier liberation
from continuing socio-political oppressions. It is often one of
their bitter experiences that the western Church seems hardly
aware of their existence or, when it does become conscious,
because of difficulties in the process of linguistic or cultural
translation that it often finds little point of comparison
between their form of Christian experience and the varieties
that are more commonly met with in the western Protestant
and Catholic Churches. Eastern Orthodoxy, claiming in a
variety of cultural forms to be the living heir of the Byzantine
religious tradition, does not wish to be seen as an exotic or
peripheral form of Christian experience; or to have its traditions described as quaint and archaic. It still lives from them
in the contemporary world. It has lived out of them in times
of great political suffering even in recent memory, proving
their power to be more than formalistically ceremonial, and it
trusts them to represent fundamental truths of the perennially
vital gospel. The sharing of that cultural religious heritage,
for purposes of mutual understanding, is something important
that may also flower into mutual religious enrichment if East
and West Christian practice and dialogue can once again have

life breathed into them, without the old ideologies and imperialisms muddying the waters.

THE SECOND ROME

One of the most intriguing things about the history of the Early Church has always been how quickly it rose from being a persecuted sect from the Orient, to taking charge of the greatest empire known to antiquity. The great persecutions of the Church (though probably there have been worse slaughters of Christians in subsequent times and places) are lodged in the collective memory as taking place in the third and fourth centuries of the Early Church. At the height of Diocletian's persecution an almost miraculous thing seemed to happen for the Christians of the empire. Constantine decided in favour of Christians. He had been educated by a Christian teacher (Lactantius) when he was a princely hostage at the court of Diocletian. To avoid being passed over in the succession of Roman emperors (his father had been appointed to the position of Western Junior Emperor) he decided to flee from the city during a purge of Christian sympathisers in 305 and to throw in his lot with the northern army based at York in England. His father was terminally ill, and on his death Constantine was acclaimed in 306 by the troops in what is now the crypt of York Minster as rightful heir and successor to the imperial title. So he began, in effect, a major civil war. In 313 he achieved a decisive victory over Maxentius, his main rival for the imperial title in the West.

Maxentius had barricaded himself behind the walls of Rome, but after choosing to meet Constantine on the field of battle outside the city, he suffered a disastrous defeat. Constantine, or perhaps more accurately, his Christian rhetoricians, Lactantius and Eusebius, depicted this battle of the 'Milvian Bridge' in terms that made it symbolically the most famous of all armed encounters in Christian history. The story was circulated that Constantine had seen (or dreamed, in one version) a great sign in the sky on the eve of his battle, and an unknown force had instructed him to draw a special heraldic device on his soldiers' shields. In this 'sign' he was promised victory. The sign he had inscribed was interpreted to him by significant church factions as none other than the cross of Christ – or at least a form of it close to the Chi-Rho, the first two letters of Christ's name which could be written in Greek in a way that drew out their similarity to the sign of the cross. From that time onwards, Constantine harnessed his star to the fortunes of the Christian Church. And the Church, which by the fourth century had risen to prominence anyway, despite numerous purges, finally came into the full light of day. When Constantine decreed reparations for the financial damages it had suffered in the past, it also became a major financial, as well as moral and political, power in the ancient systems of governance. It did not flinch from its task and the great opportunities presented to it. And so began the second stage of Christian expansion known as the Christian imperial centuries. The Church had, within four centuries from its foundation, subverted its persecutors and Christianised the empire, in the sense of seizing and holding for many centuries to come, the reins of supreme power. This was the beginning of the long process of correlating the Roman imperial traditions with the customs and practices of the Christian Church. The missionary expansion of Christianity was given an immense stimulus, and a wave of new, imperially funded, churches began to be constructed, including the first St Peter's at Rome, and the Church of the Holy Sepulchre at Jerusalem. Roman educational practices and legal prescripts were slowly harmonised with Christian premises, and long series of Christian rhetoricians and theologians (later called the Christian Fathers[5]) began the composition and accumulation of a specific body of Christian poetry, exegesis, law, and – above all – spiritual writings meant for the education and advancement of monks.

As soon as he had assumed supreme monarchical power in all the Roman dominions in 324, Constantine moved to bring the Church into play as a main element in his creation of a new state. He summoned the first worldwide, or 'ecumenical', council at Nicaea in 325, and so began a long line of imperially sponsored synods that became the standard authority of ancient Christianity seeking to clarify controversies and set out policies that would direct the universal Church. That subsequent 'oecumenical theology' is the common standard of catholicity for the western Catholic and Orthodox Churches to this day.

Taking a hard look at the lessons he had learned on his way to becoming the sole autocratic emperor of the western and eastern provinces of Rome's dominions, Constantine decided that the city of Rome had to be abandoned as a capital for an empire that had now grown far greater than anyone had originally conceived possible. So it was that he founded a new capital – the 'Second Rome', 'Queen of all Cities' – Constantinople. The new city, Christian in character from the outset (whereas Rome remained solidly pagan in its senatorial leading families for at least another generation) soon outshone the old capital in every respect. It was militarily, economically, and geographically, the true heart of the Roman world; a major port and a vastly important centre of international cultural influence. Old Rome fell into a serous decline with the eastward migration of the imperial capital, and the new Archbishop of Constantinople began to assume more and more significance: often to the irritation of the older ecclesiastical sees such as Rome or Alexandria, which frequently resulted in conflict. At the Council of Constantinople in 381 the issue of precedence was settled, with Rome being formally designated the senior see, and Constantinople ranked after it. To all intents and purposes, however, since Constantinople was the imperial city, its ecclesiastical politics were also in the ascendancy from the fourth century until the era of the Middle Ages. The city of Constantine had formerly been a small settlement in the Bosphorus called 'Byzantium'. The old term was retained and came to be a designation of the wider culture of the Greek Christian world as it revolved around Constantinople. 'Byzantine', however, is more or less a modern word.

The inhabitants of the capital at Constantinople, and all the Christians of the East who looked to the emperor, never used it as a self-reference but simply called themselves 'Romans'. They were the Empire; an Empire that God had now gifted to the Christians as his elect people. The borders of that empire, especially as they were determined by Persia to the East, and later by Islam, were regarded as the physical borders of the Kingdom of God as it had been established, so far, on earth. The defence of Rome was, in the eyes of all the Byzantines, therefore, synonymous with the protection of the flock of God, and both emperors and ecclesiastics tried to work together in achieving some kind of 'symphonia', or harmony, of Church and State affairs. The separation of Church and State was regarded more as a blasphemous concept than the ideal it has come to be in modern times. The emperor was God's anointed, like the royal Priest and King David; but although his intervention in the Church was expected, there were often serious disruptions resultant when he did so injudiciously.

Emperors such as Justinian in the sixth century tried to maintain a real, not merely a theoretical, hold over the military security of the Roman Empire's western possessions, including North Africa, Spain, and Italy. But the pressure of Germanic tribal migrations from the fourth century onwards led inevitably to the western territories bearing the brunt of social upheavals from the fourth to the seventh centuries, and by the end of that period (often symbolically posited in the reign of Pope Gregory the Great) the western parts of the empire slowly began to detach more and more from any real connection with the life and affairs of the eastern Christian Empire. Its emperor, its culture, and its ecclesiastical affairs became ever more and more legendary to the inhabitants of the West, while their cultures increasingly came to be regarded as 'barbarian' by the Byzantines themselves.

By the tenth century, pressure from the westwards migration of Islam had radically shrunk the geographical extent of the East Roman Empire, and left it with only two real cities: Constantinople and Thessalonike. Cut off from the centre and from any real hope of Byzantine military support, the Christian provinces of Palestine, Egypt, the Nile monastic communities, Nubia, Ethiopia, Armenia, Syria and Arabia, were all either overwhelmed, shrunk to a tiny fraction of themselves, or left radically isolated.

Relations between the Churches of the Byzantine world on the one hand, and the growing nation-states of the West, under the spiritual presidency of the papacy, on the other, had always tended to be difficult after the rise of Constantinople and the migration of the imperial court there. By the eleventh century they had grown very frosty indeed, and deteriorated to the point of a serious falling out in 1054 that resulted in the churches of Rome and Constantinople setting out formal condemnations (anathemas) of one another – condemnations that were only symbolically lifted by the Patriarch of Constantinople, Athenagoras, and Pope Paul VI in the mid twentieth century. The infamous Fourth Crusade of 1204 saw western Christian knights abandoning their journey to the Holy Land and instead settling for easier spoils of rape and pillage in Constantinople, amazing even themselves by the wealth gained from looting its churches and palaces. It was an event which radically embittered all subsequent church relations between the Greeks and Latins, but also permanently damaged the long-term political stability of the eastern empire.

Byzantium had a long and productive twilight, however. In the tenth century it sponsored the Christianisation of the Slavs, something that would have an immense impact on the shape of world-Christianity ever afterwards. In the eleventh century and again in the thirteenth and fourteenth centuries there were periods of great revival, at least in writing and the arts. Some of the iconography and architecture from the latter revival (the Paleologan period, so named from the dynasty of emperors then ruling) can still be seen, such as the little jewel of a church St Saviour in Chora (Kariye Jamii) in Istanbul. Even when the Ottoman armies conquered the city, in 1453, Byzantium had an afterlife in the practices and ceremonials of the Orthodox Church. Monastic colonies, founded by emperors, such as Mount Athos in Halkidiki,[6] or the Hesychast monasteries in Northern Romania,[7] still continue as if Byzantium were alive. The spiritual culture, of course, remains the dominant form of the inner life of the eastern churches to this day, with a rich and ancient tradition of saints and teachers who represent Christian writing at its zenith, at its most mystical and powerful. Many of the writings still await a translation into a modern language, but those which have witnessed an English edition in the latter part of this century soon established themselves as 'Christian classics'.

What follows in this book will be an attempt to offer an introductory guide to what those writers, poets and saints felt to be important, and of perennial value.

2. THE BEAUTY OF GOD: THE BYZANTINE THEOLOGICAL AESTHETIC

THE STRANGER OF MANTINEA

Let us begin where we wish to end: with beauty. This is perhaps a demanding and over-abstract beginning for such a short book of introduction, but no concept so summates the ethos or guiding cultural spirit of eastern Christianity as much as that perennial search for beauty which inspired and organised the Byzantine mystical quest. As such it is something that, as a 'master-theme', will illuminate our understanding of all those disparate 'avenues' to spiritual insight which comprise those concepts that represent our subsequent chapters, whether these deal with monastic literature, poetry, hagiographies, or liturgy. The synonymity of beauty and holiness is something that resonates throughout all Byzantine religious philosophy, emerging time and time again, even into the present Orthodox world. Prince Myshkin's exclamation in Dostoevsky's novel *The Idiot* catches the idea exactly: 'Beauty will save the World!'[1] In its theory of beauty Christian Byzantium tried to marry the highest and best insights of Greek philosophy with the biblical conception of the merciful Creator who redeems and transfigures the creation at every turn. The Byzantine starting point was to seek a common language of discourse with Greek philosophical thought on the nature of the good and the true. Accordingly, Plato was almost like an Old Testament prophet – foreshadowing the truth Christ was later to reveal clearly.

In a significant essay on the nature of Platonic philosophy,

R.J. O'Connell highlights one of the most interesting and prob-
lematic aspects of the identification of the good and the
beautiful in the pre-Christian Greek philosophical tradition:

> It is a truism to say that, for the Greek mind, the good
> and the beautiful (*kalokagathon*) are at one, just as the
> evil and the ugly are. Use these terms in their moral
> sense, however, and the gigantic act of 'belief' implied in
> that equivalence becomes more evident.[2]

The widespread and distinctive Greek idea that moral utility
(what was good by virtue of being beneficial) would coincide
with socially accepted senses of rightness of action,[3] was an
idea that sounded well, and sometimes worked, but was frequently doomed to failure as a standard of ethics in so far as
it did not have the workaday capacity to make sense of those
many situations of moral conflict that called for a good action
that brought no benefit to its agent. Many can be the occasions
when one is called upon to do the 'right thing', to do one's
duty, when the result is far from beneficial or advantageous.
To the simple idea of utilitarian 'goodness' in early Greek
thought Socrates brought a more refined and transcendent
notion of aesthetics. To this Plato remained faithful.

In an important section of his *Symposium*, and in other
dialogues such as the *Phaedrus*, Plato's sense of the moral
beauty of an act, which had to take precedence over any questions of its advantageousness, advanced Greek thought into a
new realm of moral awareness – one that had begun to take
seriously the issue of moral beauty as such. For Plato belief
that the beautiful and the good would coincide, still remained
an act of faith, but a faith that was now grounded on a more
robust realism. When the two forces of utility and virtue did
not apparently or immediately coincide, then the precedence
was unquestioningly given to the moral beauty of an act.
Knowing that this preference could only be sustained on the
ground of an enduring fundamental trust that however difficult the resolution might be, nevertheless the good and the
true must be ultimately one, Plato held that the perception of

this ultimate unity was a call to an ascending purification of perception, one that was religiously inspired and indeed no less than the transcendental imperative. Such an idea was one of the great forward leaps in the history of human thought and, even for this insight alone, justified the sense entertained by several of the fathers (and certainly some of the Byzantine church painters who delighted in iconically depicting Plato on the narthex walls as a precursor of the gospel) that here was a tradition of thought and belief that, like the Jewish lawyer, was 'not far from the Kingdom of God'.

Plato added more: he understood that such a purified perception, frequently running against the current of human needs and self-referent desires, needed a dynamic motivating force to realise it, and, accordingly, posited love as the supreme virtue, or force, that gave the moral aesthetic sense its transcendent dynamic. In his *Symposium* he attributes the key role of teacher of these mysteries to the 'stranger of Mantinea', the priestess Diotima. In and through her initiations Plato intimates the profoundly religious character of his insight that the person who habitually prefers beauty is thereby increasingly led to an ascent to the Supremely Beautiful:

> Whoever has been instructed so far in the things of love, and who has learned to see the beautiful in due order and succession, when they come to the end will suddenly perceive a nature of wondrous beauty . . . beauty absolute, separate, simple, and everlasting, which is imparted to the ever-growing and transient beauties of all other beautiful things, without itself suffering diminution, or increase, or any change. Whoever ascends from these earthly things under the influence of true love, and begins to perceive *that* beauty, is not far from the end. And the true order of progress, or rather the manner of being led by another, to the things of love, is to begin from the beauties of this world and mount upwards for the sake of that other beauty, using these things merely as steps; and from one going on to two, and from two to all fair bodily forms,

and from fair bodily forms to fair practices, and from
fair practices to fair sciences, until from fair sciences one
arrives at the science of which I have spoken, the science
which has no other object than absolute beauty, and we
can at last know that which is beautiful by itself alone.
This, my dear Socrates, said the stranger of Mantinea, is
that life above all others which a human ought to live out,
in the contemplation of beauty absolute . . . But what if a
person had eyes to see the true beauty, – the divine beauty
I mean, pure and clear and all unalloyed, not infected
with the defilements of the flesh and all the colours and
vanities of mortal life, – rather, looking, and holding con-
verse with the true beauty simple and divine? Remember
how in that communion only, beholding beauty with that
by which it can be beheld,[4] such a one will be enabled to
bring forth not images of beauty, but realities (for then we
have hold not of an image but of a reality) and such a
person could then demonstrate and develop true virtue,
and then will truly become the friend of God and become
immortal, if mortal kind ever may . . .[5]

PLATO'S INFLUENCE ON ORIGEN

This passage was to have a profound effect on the Christian
consciousness and formed a strong link between the Hellenistic
philosophical and Christian Byzantine traditions in later centuries. In this justly famous speech of the 'stranger of
Mantinea' Plato's theory of the Ideal Forms takes on a status
that is more than the merely ideational, and gives him the
basis for a moral teleology. His progress towards this insight
can be traced in the course of his writings.

In his dialogue *Meno* Plato begins his theory of Ideal Forms
from the basis of a theory of knowledge: thus we do not
approach truth by deductive processes based on sensory reality
(*aisthesis*), rather we intuitively recollect the truth in so far
as we have already experienced it before birth in a purely
Noetic[6] form (*noetikos, anaisthetos*). This starting point of the

theory of knowledge is important to keep in mind, but the Theory of Ideals extends its significance in other works of Plato into the metaphysical or cosmological domain. The theory of knowledge, if kept in tandem with the theory of Forms, preserves the character of the Platonic Cosmos as a moral teleology. In the *Symposium* where the Ideal Form of Beauty is most clearly argued, this teleology attains the character of an aesthetic, which transfigures into ethic and, ultimately, into mysticism. This triadic process, from its roots in Plato's religious sense of the Beautiful, bears the character of an ascent, an ascent articulated most fully in religious terms, as we have seen, in the speech of Diotima in the *Symposium*.

The significance of this dynamic of ascent, and its relationship with Christianity, has long been categorised as one of the results of the impact of NeoPlatonic ideas on the Church, especially in the period of the fifth century after Plotinos and Augustine. But the tendency to centralise the philosophical *telos* (end-goal) as the ascent of the soul to the Transcendent Absolute is already the major concern of the Middle Platonists of the early Christian era. As such, it is a dominant concern of one of the more famous of that school – the Christian philosopher Origen of Alexandria. Through him the Platonic notion of ascent is fundamentally moderated in its shape by the twin stimuli of Christian Logos-theology and biblical exegesis, and through him it comes very early on, and most powerfully, into the Christian mystical tradition. This Origenian strand continues to emphasise the Platonic insight that the ecstatic perception of Beauty is the highest perception of truth afforded to creatures. Origen's *Commentary on the Song of Songs* demonstrates the notion clearly, and had a marked impact on Christian spirituality in both East and West thereafter.

Origen's legacy was most notably developed in the classical Byzantine patristic era (fourth to sixth centuries) by Gregory Nazianzen (The Theologian), Gregory of Nyssa, Evagrios Pontike, Dionysios the Pseudo-Areopagite, and Maximos the Confessor. All of them, in their own way, diffract and mediate Origen's own style of theorising, in the process of articulating a fully-fledged and particularly Christian approach to the problem. After this it is no longer accurate to speak of Platonised Christianity, or Christianised Platonism, for neither reduction does justice to the unique synthesis which the Byzantine Christian paradigm represents: something which the Russian theologian Florovsky[7] wished to designate (in deliberate antithesis to the liberal Protestant historian Adolf Von Harnack[8]) as the 'Christianisation of Hellenism'. It remains true, however, that the Origenian tradition, even when subjected to such a masterly synthesis as that offered by the Cappadocian Fathers, remains far stronger in articulating the ascent from flesh to spiritual perception than it is in describing the transfiguration of materiality which lay outside the ken of Plato, and was reserved as a mystery of the incarnation. It is this constant grounding of Origen's mystical insight that the later Byzantine tradition represents, not a turning away from Origen and Plato's mystical insights, but a demand that their fulfilment lay within, not apart from, the transfiguration of flesh and all materiality that had been consummated in the incarnation of the Logos of God in the person of Jesus the Christ. The ascetical tradition of such as Makarios, and the typical praxis of asceticism of the other monastic teachers such as Pachomios, Shenoude, Euthymios, Saba, and John Climakos, played an important synthetic role in this regard, all of them representing varieties of influence on a theology of transcendentalist aesthetics in the Origenian aftermath.

THE CONCILIAR PATRISTIC TRADITION

The Church's major Christological conflicts from the fourth to the fifth centuries also produced a significant body of thought, from such as Athanasios and Cyril, that added to the simpler monastic and moral tradition, and which also grounded its mystical endeavour in an incarnational theology of revelation and *theosis*.[9] This was a high conciliar approach that was partly indebted to Origen but in significant aspects wholly independent of him and more affirmative of the body and sacramental materiality than ever he would care to be. From Cyril of Alexandria onwards we can definitively recognise an authentic Christology of 'transfigured materiality': a major divergence from Plato's theology of the mystical transcendence of materiality. Cyril's Christological images of the lily and its perfume representing the union of divine and human in Christ, or the bond of soul and body representing the manner of the incarnation of the divine in history, perfectly sum up this newly sharpened sense of 'transfiguration theology'.[10]

MAXIMOS THE CONFESSOR AND DIONYSIOS THE AREOPAGITE

This double aspect and character of the genuinely Christian theological concern – namely, the apprehension of God as the Absolute Beauty drawing the soul onward in ecstasy, and the approach to the divine encounter in Christ as the transfiguration of matter, ultimately finds both its polarities reconciled in the late Byzantine synthesis. Maximos already demonstrates this, as does Dionysios the Pseudo-Areopagite. Their treatment of theological aesthetics marks them out as dependent on Plato's insight, while simultaneously developing it in a thoroughly Christianised form into new dimensions: a 'sea-change' into something rich and strange. Maximos, in the following passage, demonstrates a masterly synthesis of Plato and the biblical tradition of the image and its relation to the divine archetype when he speaks of entering into the Archetypal Beauty in terms of Noetic initiation:

> When Moses pitches his tent outside the camp (Ex. 33:7), that is when he establishes his will and mind outside the world of visible things, then it is that he begins to worship God. Then, entering into the darkness (Ex. 20:21), that is into the formless and immaterial realm of spiritual knowledge, he celebrates there the most sacred rites. The darkness is that formless, immaterial, and bodiless state which embraces the knowledge of the prototypes of all

created things. He who like another Moses enters into it, although mortal by nature, understands things that are immortal. Through this knowledge he depicts in himself the beauty of divine excellence, as if painting a picture which is a faithful copy of Archetypal Beauty. Then he comes down from the mountain and offers himself as an example to those who wish to imitate that excellence. In this way he manifests the love and generosity of the grace he has received.[11]

Here, the conception of the highest level of mystical union does not abandon materiality, but descends, like Moses from Sinai, and (though unstated, the parallel is certainly implied) like the Logos from heaven. This is a descent which no longer in any sense can be understood as a decline. It is a *katabasis* of mercy, a stooping down in the biblical sense, like a mother in tenderness coming down to her child. It is a descent of the 'Economy' – a coming down to save which is the heart of the dynamic of God's liberative revelation, which Maximos also sees as prefiguring the *parousia*. In this eschatological sense *katabasis* is also given as a duty to disciples (in that interval of time and space which belongs to them as Church) for their own 'stooping in mercy' to the world after they have encountered the mystery of their Lord is the very essence of the economy of the Church's mission in the world – the Church's fundamental and inalienable duty to witness the truth, to proclaim the gospel across time and space.

For Maximos, the descent does not dissipate the power of the vision, rather it manifests it in love and mercy in an economy of the transfigured life. This is a recurring dynamic of *katabasis* and *anabasis* (ascending and descending) based on the pattern of the Logos' own ascent and descent as described by the Evangelist John.

Maximos and Dionysios are the two Christian theorists who apply reflection on the Greek spiritual notion of the *kalokagathon*[12] most explicitly. Maximos does so in another passage which demonstrates his careful reading of Plato; and yet Plato could never have written as this great Christian mystic does. It remains a mystery why so many commentators regard such a passage as evidence of a thoroughly 'Platonised' Christian consciousness (usually understood in a pejorative sense) when even the most diffident comparison of this with Diotima's speech should reveal to anyone who has the eyes to see or the ears to hear, the profoundly different emphases that Maximos' apprehension of the gospel imperatives has brought to the fore. Here is Plato's insight, certainly, but subordinated in a powerful Christian confession to the overriding providence of a personal power of Love that seeks to redeem its creatures even to the point of divine *kenosis*:[13]

[83]. The Beautiful is identical with The Good, for all things seek the beautiful and the good at every opportunity, and there is no being that does not participate in them. They extend to all that is, being whatever is truly admirable, sought for, desired, pleasing, chosen and loved. Observe how the divine force of love – that power of Eros pre-existing in the Good – has given birth to the same blessed force within us, through which we long for the beautiful and the good in accordance with the words, 'I became a lover of her beauty' (WS 8:2) and, 'Love her and she will sustain you; fortify her and she will exalt you' (Prov. 4:6,8).

[84]. Theologians call the divine, sometimes an erotic force, sometimes love, sometimes that which is intensely longed-for and loved.[14] Consequently, as an erotic force, and as love, the divine itself is subject to movement; and as that which is intensely longed-for and loved, it moves towards itself everything that is receptive of this force and love. To express this more clearly: the divine itself is subject to movement since it produces an inward state of intense longing and love in those who are receptive to this, and it moves others since by its very nature it attracts the desire of those who are drawn towards it. In other words, it moves

others and itself moves, since it thirsts to be thirsted for, longs to be longed-for, and loves to be loved.

[86]. One must also, in the name of truth, be bold enough to affirm that the Cause of All Things, through the beauty, goodness, and profusion of his intense love for everything, goes out of himself in his providential care for the whole of creation. By means of the supra-essential power of ecstasy, and spell-bound as it were by goodness, love, and longing, he relinquishes his utter transcendence in order to dwell in all things while yet remaining within himself. Hence, those skilled in divine matters call him a zealous and exemplary lover, because of the intensity of his blessed longing for all things, and because he rouses others to imitate his own intense desire, revealing himself as their exemplar.[15]

Maximos has not only baptised Plato in this classical Byzantine synthesis, he has also brought home the wild genius of his teacher Origen, and harmonised the latter's visions of the truth and his clear-sighted glimpse of the transcendent divine beauty, with the Church's more developed theology of the sacramental nature of the divine incarnation. This, of course, was Maximos' double intent from the outset.

THE BYZANTINE PERCEPTION OF BEAUTY

Why have we begun here? Why take the notion of the beautiful as our starting point in a consideration of the Byzantine spiritual tradition? I think for two reasons. In the first place the initial chapter needs to stand in some sense, as an introductory gateway to the whole. Of all the possible attempts to capture an overriding 'ethos' of Byzantine spirituality, it seems to me that one would be best served by entering through the gate of the Beautiful, and such a gate, in East Christian thought, always opens out into the Court of the Divine. Many books about East Christian mysticism traditionally begin with the major significance of Logos theology on the Greek mind. Such classics as Vladimir Lossky's *The Mystical Theology of the Eastern Church*, or that other modern masterpiece by Olivier Clément, *The Roots of Christian Mysticism*, both demonstrate that pathway. To approach the aspect of Byzantine spirituality from the vantage point of a theology of aesthetics does not contradict the essential truth that Logos Mysticism encapsulates the whole, but sets the same thing in a slightly different light, and from that different colouration emerge some different planes of the picture as we study it holistically. This was my second motivation – to highlight why I think Byzantine spirituality is important, and more than important, essential to a Christian's self understanding.

The term 'Byzantine spirituality' needs some explanation, partly because the concept of spirituality, and books of spirituality, are often accused today of being the 'soft-centre' of Christian thought in an age that has lost its grip of the fundamentals; and partly because 'Byzantine' (as we saw earlier) had been so prejudicially treated in parts of the western consciousness that it was used to signify labyrinthine duplicity, or at the very least something 'exotic and strange' that by its very oddity is justly relegated to the peripheries. These presumptions are not merely wrong, but so wrong that they become dangerously misleading, and can blind one to the simple reality that the Byzantine tradition of Christianity is far from an exotic hot-house bloom, simply a way that Christians from ancient times have struggled to live out the gospel calling. If one of the fundamental insights of that tradition of spirituality is that the gospel has something profound to do with beauty and culture, then it not only has obvious implications in the historic creation, say, of a particularly 'Byzantine Christian consciousness' (the continuing tradition of the Orthodox churches) but also in the call to examine the cultural underpinnings of faith, and the manner in which Christian faith has the responsibility to inform and change human culture. In an era when ordinary men and women are increasingly speaking about post-Christian societies, this task of examining the root fundamentals has never been more urgent. And in this task the Byzantine theology of spiritual aesthetics has an important and central role to play.

The times demand that the Church looks once more at its mystical and philosophical tradition in a world and an era where the two notions have suffered a fatal divorce in the so-called 'post Christian' context. But why should theological aesthetics be repositioned as one of the most important areas of contemporary theology, calling out for attention and development, even though it is now largely relegated to the sidelines and often misunderstood as an exercise in 'cosmetics' (the secular Greek word for peripheral beautification)? It is my belief that here, in the theology of Beauty,[16] is an agenda for twenty-first-century theology that will rescue the discipline from its tendency to concentrate increasingly on the ephemeral or the purely socio-historical in its growing anxiety that its voice is becoming less and less relevant to contemporary society. Byzantine theology, which once dealt so well with the same problems of communicating a vision of truth that was somehow at once familiar and yet new to its contemporary world, has an important role to play in this process of intellectual brokering and hermeneutics. It cannot do this, however, if either as an intellectual tradition, or an ecclesial tradition of mysticism, it is imprisoned in the domain of the merely historical or archival.

Byzantine mystical spirituality characteristically, and paradoxically, demands to be approached as a practical life-discipline. It is a vision of the highest beauty that begins in the processes of bodily orientation, forms of prayer, and even eating habits. The Eastern Church's deep-rooted tradition of a mystical and sacramental understanding of God that is at one and the same time securely founded on a moral apprehension of self-sacrificing virtue as the Supremely Beautiful (the religion of the Incarnate Lord), is a supreme remedy (*pharmakeion*) offered to a radically secularised society that has progressively weakened its old harmony of religion and culture to the point where it has become soft on rationality, soft on ethics, soft on justice, and soft on truth.

THE PROCLAMATION OF BEAUTY TO A NEEDY WORLD

For a society that is in danger of losing even the distant memories of its root religious civilisation, at a time when its preferred religions have shrunk back in the face of serious social decline, and its schools of political, philosophical, and artistic thought have elevated short-term self-interest to new heights, the Church's task is no less than to show the way back to a renewed sense of the Beautiful. It will be in the Christian reinterpretation of the Greek notion of *kalokagathon*, no less than the ideal synthesis of a religious, mystical, and moral transcendental. It is, if the Church can still act decisively enough to be the intellectual midwife and interpreter, the one concept and experience that can still be remembered well enough by a generally 'paganised' society to serve as the basis for a new pro-paideusis[17] of what civilisation and human aspirations to ascent are all about. If the Church can find the wit, and the energy, for the task, then this pro-paideusis will be no less than a re-evangelisation of the western world, which has already declined far from its former and higher standards of religious civilisation, and now urgently needs catechising about the very nature of the simplest truths – what constitutes Beauty; and where lies the reconciliation of Aesthetics and Justice – central ideas constitutive to a civilisation that even a few decades ago might have been thought to be hardly capable of being forgotten in so short a time and so widespread a fashion.

In brief, the theology of Beauty, one of the great jewels in the Byzantine mystical tradition, is far from being played out. It remains to have perhaps its greatest role ever in the history of the Church. If this small book can serve in some way to demonstrate how Christian voices from the past, men and women who lived in similarly fragmented and pagan societies to ours, creatively witnessed to the Great Beauty in their own lives, and in so doing demonstrated the self-evident authenticity and integrity of the gospel they were called to proclaim in a darkened and darkening world, then it will have served a greater purpose than that of a mere historical survey. Perhaps the Byzantine spiritual tradition, forced by conquest and oppression for so many centuries to wander in the deserts, may once again fulfil a historical evangelical task, if it can lead others from the obscurities to the illumined places where the mysteries are celebrated 'with unveiled faces'. Socrates' friend, the priestess of Mantinea, was perfectly right: such a journey to the Beautiful can only be made if one who has seen leads by the hand, with care and love, the one who desires to see. For such a great and pressing destiny, we must be ready. We must be ready too to listen to those voices of the tradition who have:

> ... seen with our eyes, have gazed upon, have touched with our hands – the Word of Life, which was made manifest and which we have seen and bear witness in our turn to you – that Life Eternal which was with the Father and has now been manifested to us. (1 John 1:1–2).

3. AN IMAGELESS VISION: EVAGRIOS PONTIKE

EVAGRIOS THE SEEKER

Origen was the Christian thinker who, more than all others, worked to bring Plato's vision of divine beauty into harmony with the gospel of Christ; but it was to be a disciple of his in the next generation, Evagrios Pontike, who served to develop that legacy most as it related to the spiritual life, and the doctrine of prayer. Evagrios lived between 345 and 399.[1] He was the son of a village bishop, a native of Ibora in Pontus, the Black Sea region of the coast of modern Turkey. He became a disciple of the Cappadocian Fathers, Basil the Great, Gregory of Nazianzus, and Gregory of Nyssa. Gregory Nazianzen taught him rhetoric as a young man, Basil appointed him a church lector, and Gregory Nyssa ordained him as a deacon. In 380 he came to Constantinople to assist Gregory Nazianzen in composing a famous series of Orations demonstrating the divinity of the three persons of the Trinity.[2] This was the immediate prelude to the Council of Constantinople of 381 whose trinitarian creed became the fundamental structure of orthodoxy for the eastern and western Churches: the creed that is still recited in the eucharistic services of the Greek and Latin Churches today. Shortly after the Council, Evagrios had to flee from the city, having been involved with an aristocratic woman and rousing the murderous jealousy of the lady's husband against him. His hagiographer, Palladios, euphemistically tries to soften the 'scandal' into a case of guilty dreams and a vow of repentance. In disgrace he wandered as far as Jerusalem where he met with a noble Roman lady, Melania, who gave him hospitality in her monastery on the Mount of Olives, and encouraged him to see in his disgrace the providential marks of God's special election: he should go off to the desert in Egypt and there become a solitary monk. He took the advice of these learned ascetics with the utmost seriousness, and so it was that one of the brightest scholars of his generation, a young aristocrat who had been accustomed to the society of the most learned philosophers and theologians of his day, in 383 asked to be received in the peasant communities of monks in the desert area of Nitria, higher up the Nile from Egyptian Alexandria. He stayed at Nitria for two years, then in 385 moved on to the famous hermit colonies of nearby Kellia, further into the desert, and stayed there until his death. He joined a community of intelligentsia monks under the leadership of Ammonios, one of the so-called 'Tall Brothers', the leaders of the Origenistic monks of Egypt. Their monastic family was soon called the 'household of Ammonios and Evagrios', later simply the 'house of Evagrios' as his own reputation as a master of the inner life and a skilled interpreter of human psychology became widely known. In the desert he met two of the most eminent spiritual masters of the day, the two Makarii, one of whom was a priest at Kellia, and the other a monk whom he sometimes visited to hear his teachings given at the monastic colony of Scete. He himself was visited by the Greek chronicler Palladios who took his name and reputation back to the imperial city when he composed his Lausiac History,[3] which he wrote to describe what he had found on his travels through Egyptian monasticism. The Greek world recognised Evagrios even in his lifetime as an internationally significant writer, but there is some evidence of friction with local Coptic monks who resented him as a *xenos* (a foreigner) who was introducing strange and alien ideas (Platonic philosophy) into the simple monastic lifestyle that had hitherto characterised the communities of the desert. The celebrated stories in the 'Sayings of the Desert Fathers' making the point that all of Evagrios' learning could not compare to the simple and holy asceticism of the old ascetics[4] should not be taken as evidence that the desert monks in general despised the Greek intellectual because they were themselves 'simple peasants', for the source of these apparently disparaging sayings is certainly Evagrios himself, employing his characteristic modesty and tact. The common image of the majority of Egyptian monks as uneducated peasantry is certainly not an accurate one.

Whereas, like his teacher Gregory Nazianzus, Evagrios was a devoted follower of Origen, he was noticeably less careful than Gregory in moderating some of the speculative side of his hero, particularly the notion that souls came to earth from a pre-existent state and that their fall into materiality was part of their punishment for pre-earthly crimes. When he stayed in Jerusalem he found in Melania and her associate, the theologian Rufinus, two dedicated Origenists with a marked interest in applying the teacher's doctrine in the domain of mystical prayer. Rufinus was engaged at this period in translating Origen's works into Latin, and it is certain that Evagrios renewed his study of Origen at this time. What he did with the old master that was distinct and new, was to focus Origen's metaphysic precisely onto the praxis of an individual's ascetic and mystical ascent, thus making this kind of 'theology' profoundly relevant to the burgeoning desert movement, and to Christian asceticism in general. This could be argued, historically speaking, to be the archetypal moment of the founding of Christian mystical theology, as a discipline.

Evagrios followed Origen in teaching that the spiritual *nous* of each living person (that is the spiritual intellect, or the essential spiritual identity of a person) had been created pure in a pre-cosmic state, but had fallen. This lapse from God separated out Souls, dividing up the once unanimous body of Spirits (the angels around God's throne[5]). After the fall, God created the world as a penitentiary to assist the lapsed Souls to purify themselves prior to their spiritual ascent back to the heavenly regions.

The escape from the body was an important part of the return to true identity, though Evagrios was careful to insist that the body per se was not an evil thing or a punishment. It was rather our God-given means of spiritual ascent,[6] the vehicle with which and through which the eternal soul could rise up once again to spiritual glory. Accordingly the ascetic had to treat the body with great respect, though equally the body was a merely temporary medium, and had to be disciplined so that it could effectively serve as the means of spiritual focus rather than the cause of sensual dissipation. This true spiritual identity, the *nous*, was destined to ascend from the earth, but had to purify itself from earthly limitations. God, as an absolute spirit, could not be approached by bodily means. For Evagrios the purification of the senses by strict asceticism, and the training of the mind to transcend the limits of the flesh, were paramount factors in allowing the ascetic or monk to return to the spiritual state from which the soul or *nous* had declined.

His overt Origenism (which in turn depended heavily on Plato's understanding of the uneasy dwelling of an eternal consciousness within a temporary fleshly medium) made several of his contemporaries very anxious indeed, worrying how such apparent dualism could be reconciled with the strongly incarnational spirit of Christianity. While Evagrios devoted his time as a monk to elucidating his metaphysic in terms of spiritual writings, many of the monks in the surrounding Egyptian region began to make loud complaints against him. While he was alive Theophilos, the powerful Archbishop of Alexandria, more or less protected him, but immediately after his death the Archbishop joined in with the forces of opposition that were mounting and so began a purge of Evagrios' memory and writings, instigating a much larger movement aimed at eradicating Platonic influence from Christian thought: the attack against 'Origenism'.[7]

As a result of the ecclesiastical condemnations which began in his lifetime and reached their peak in Evagrios' formal censure at the Second Council of Constantinople in 552, his works were scattered and most have been lost. But even after his official condemnation Evagrios remained a darling of the monastic movement. The monks who read him were not willing to allow such an insightful and stimulating author to be lost without trace and so, by subterfuge, several of his main spiritual writings were saved, listed under the name of other authors such as the suitably obscure 'St Nilos', or simply surviving in Syriac translation, to be rediscovered in the twentieth century. His practical writings especially lived on as a main platform for the ever-growing ascetic movement.

THE MASTER OF THE PRACTICAL

Evagrios was not only the most speculative and noetic of all the Byzantine writers but, paradoxically, the most eminently insightful practitioner too, giving intimate psychological analysis and advice in his texts. For this reason his practical writings survived intact, and continued to exercise an influence on those intellectuals who pushed further to read and try to comprehend his Origenian insights. Evagrios was the real founder of a technical vocabulary in Christian spiritual writing, and all subsequent writing on spirituality is indebted to him for this, and also for his theoretical division of the spiritual life into three stages of progress: the practical fight against passions that marks the beginning stages of prayer, the growing fervour and understanding of the middle stage of a serious spiritual seeker, and the increasingly 'wordless' state of the mystical union with God. He is not a specially 'systematic' writer, as most of his works have the character of oral teaching written up in the form of 'particular issues', but while his writings show no overarching coherence, one can clearly discern in his major works a kind of threefold progression: issues of the ascetical life and temptations, questions related to the practice of prayer, and speculative 'higher knowledge' questions. The instruction is designed to rise in complexity depending on the level of experience of the monastic disciple. This threefold ascent can be seen in his three main works: *Praktikos*, *Chapters on Prayer*, and *Gnostic Chapters*. It was the latter volume, highly speculative and metaphysical in tone that called down the condemnations of the Fifth Oecumenical Council in 553.

Taking Origen's suggestions on ascetical life, but consciously trying to make them more approachable in the form of a manual for ascetics, Evagrios divided the Christian life into three essential stages of growth: three characteristic activities. The first was *praktike*: the practical stage of learning how to cultivate the necessary virtues. It is a laborious stage, particularly suited to new monks who attempt to avoid common sins and become master of their desires as they live a disciplined life dedicated to the goals of purification and extended prayer. The second stage develops alongside the first, as an intellectual corollary to it. This is *physike*: the contemplation of created realities – to increase the capacity for intellective comprehension. It is a form of noetic askesis, the training and control of the psychic and intellective imagination, whereas *praktike* is largely concerned with physical ascetical exercises and verbal prayer forms. The third and highest stage is that of *theologike*. This can only be embarked on when some progress has been made on the two prior stages. It amounts to the awesome approach to the knowledge of God, and increasingly takes on the character of a wordless, imageless incomprehensibility. The higher the spiritual teachings, the less comprehensible they will be to those who have had no prior experience. Evagrios' higher teachings were reserved for his close circle of disciples and deliberately become increasingly speculative and obscure. The higher the experience of God becomes, the more accurately it mirrors the divine incomprehensibility, and the less it becomes capable of expression in human linguistic or ideational forms. From being initially ekphrastic (having an ability to be expressed, as in scripture or prayer, for example) it becomes increasingly apophatic (beyond the capacity of language, inexpressible), and thereby increasingly a mystical intuition of the incomprehensibly Transcendent One. Any image offered by the mind, at this stage of prayer, has to be misleading and illusory by its very nature.

His works are commonly in the form of *kephalaia*: a word

that literally means 'chapters' or 'short headings', a form of
ancient instructional writing that consists of disconnected pro-
positions. Like other teachers of his time Evagrios wished to
veil his more elevated discourses. The *theologike* would probably have been given to an inner circle in the form of esoteric
knowledge. The *praktike* teachings are more open, simple, and
clear. They were widely appreciated in ancient and medieval
Christianity. This was his pro-paideusis, which in fact made
his international reputation.

Evagrios' practical doctrine stresses the need for acute
psychological self-examination and clarity of analysis. He
speaks much on the rising of multitudes of thoughts (*logismoi*)
unbidden within us, which reflect our fallen variegated human
psychic condition – our alienation from the One, lost in the
vagaries of the Many. Askesis purifies the body, and spiritual
askesis (especially psalmody and monologistic prayer,[8] and the
mulling over of aphorisms) has the effect of stilling and slowing
the activities of the *logismoi*. Noetic philosophy and contemplation (*physike*) lead on to higher comprehensions.

Evagrios advocates the monastic lifestyle, and all of his writings presuppose an audience of dedicated monastic disciples:

> The monk must be the soldier of Christ, detached from
> material things, free from worldly cares, and not involved
> in any trade or commerce as the apostle teaches (2 Tim.
> 2:4). Let the monk follow this path, especially since he has
> renounced the materiality of this world in order to win
> the blessings of spiritual quietness. For the practice of
> quietness is full of joy and beauty: its yoke is easy and its
> burden light.[9]

The early stages of monastic commitment are like preparing
the ground for a crop to be sown. The renunciation of evil
marks the disciple's turning away from the principalities and
powers (the evil spirits) that constantly seek to entangle souls
while in the earthly condition. For Evagrios the demonology
of the New Testament was something quite literal. The spiritual life was a constant battle with unseen spiritual powers.

The psychological desires of the desert monks, for comfort in food or sex, were not regarded as 'natural' longings, but rather the evidence of a disordered force hostile to spiritual seekers that constantly sought means to lead them astray and confuse the goal of a life devoted to God. In Evagrios, demonology and a close psychological scrutiny of the self go hand in hand. He advocated the monastic practice of expressing all one's thoughts, even the most shameful, obscure or phantastic, to a more experienced spiritual guide. In order to help his monks recognise the complexity (and waywardness) of the inner thoughts, he devoted much writing to classifying the different types that arose in the heart and mind. First came the thought, the *logismos*. Some of these were natural, and some were inspired by demonic craftiness. If the monk dwelt on the thought it grew in strength, taking control of the intellectual life and demanding an embodiment in action. The demons inspired every evil thought that, once entertained by the monk, would inevitably produce an evil deed, corrupting the heart and banishing the Spirit of God from the temple of the heart. Evagrios offers chapters describing the typical ways each of the demons manages to insinuate its particular vice into the heart of the monk. This careful listing of the various demons and the description of their tactics to inspire their own specialist 'vices' made his work invaluable as a self-help psychological guide for solitaries anxious to understand themselves and make progress, beyond the crippling limits of their individual neuroses.

CATALOGUING THE PSYCHE

Evagrios became famous for his taxonomy of the 'eight passionate thoughts': gluttony, lust, avarice, depression, anger, world-weariness, self-opinionatedness, and pride.[10] The passions render the spirit dull, and in this way manage to make it unfit for the act of prayer.[11] All of them rose from the initial stage of the thought (*logismos*) that gave them birth in the body. In prayer it was essential to stop the thought gaining any grip. These *logismoi* were like teeming multitudes of voices, all clamouring for attention. Deprived of attention they grew faint. Only by controlling the thoughts could a spiritual life advance. Evagrios recommends:

> Reading of sacred literature, night-long vigils, and persevering prayer to lend stability to the vacillating mind. Hunger, hard toil, and solitude are the means of extinguishing the flames of desire. Soul-darkening anger can be calmed by the singing of the psalms, by penitence, and by almsgiving. But you need to put all these things into practice in good order and at the right time, otherwise it will be an erratic and short-lived response, and this will cause more harm than good.[12]

The goal of askesis, or the discipline of controlling these thoughts, was *hesychia*, spiritual stillness, where the mind (the *nous*) was able to enter a state of spiritual acuity that was almost *contra naturam* – or at least certainly beyond the 'natural' capacity of an undisciplined human mind. After the spiritual fall, stillness (the stasis of a fixed condition and a pure perception) was denied the human being. The soul was condemned in the body to suffer a myriad of humiliating distractions. Nothing was clear, direct, or straight. Only if *hesychia* could be achieved again could the *nous* in a human being function once more as if it were a pure spirit, with undimmed and clear perception of the workings of God, and a direct line between wishing to know God and a sure progress in the divine life – a path that was generally far from direct in normal conditions. For Evagrios, the highest form of spiritual stillness that was possible for the experienced monk, was *apatheia* (dispassionateness): the state of soul when bodily temptations and distractions no longer have the force to turn away the human consciousness from God. This goal of contemplation is not a luxury for the few; on the contrary, for Evagrios it was the central goal and purpose of all creaturely existence, no less than the reconciliation of the divine and the human: 'The Kingdom of Heaven is the state when the soul achieves

transcendence of passions (apatheia), and gains a clear knowledge of the order of things.'[13] For a beginner in the spiritual life,
it was the *logismoi* that prevented this pure state of spiritual
awareness,[14] which needed to be controlled firstly by physical
asceticism. Deprivation of sleep, food, and external distractions
were greatly important (hence the preference for desert caves).
No monk could advance in the paths of prayer without regular,
and rigorous fasting:

> Keep to a sparse and plain diet, not seeking a variety of
> tempting dishes. Should the thought of rich foods come to
> you under the pretext of offering hospitality, for example,
> dismiss it; do not be deceived by it, for here the Enemy
> lies in ambush waiting to tear you away from stillness.[15]

> A monk cannot drive away passionate thoughts unless he
> watches over the desires and appetites of the heart. He
> can destroy desire through fasting, vigils, and sleeping on
> the ground, and he can tame the appetites of the heart
> through long-suffering, forbearance, forgiveness, and acts
> of compassion. For almost all the demonic powers are
> connected to these two particular passions, and they lead
> the Nous to disaster and perdition if unchecked.[16]

Manual labour was also important, to keep the monk busied.
In the evenings, repetitive tasks (such as weaving or carving)
were particularly useful in keeping the body absorbed, like
a restless child, while the mind quietly focused on spiritual
thoughts. In times of prayer the same approach could be
applied, with the monk beginning with many physical prostrations (falling onto the ground full length in adoration of
God), and then the recitation of many psalms or prayers, until
such time as the mind was ready to ascend into quietness. For
beginners the physical prostrations and psalms could take up
the majority of the time of prayer, while for those more
advanced and skilled, a few psalms would bring the soul
quickly into the presence of God where it needed no thoughts
or words or images to stabilise it. When the soul was pulled

back into the whirl of the distracting *logismoi* the cycle would begin all over again. Many of the monks, following Evagrios' advice, spent long hours through the nights in the practice of prayer.

Evagrios advocated the control of anger, and the practice of gentle charity, as two of the most important prerequisites for successful prayer. Without loving gentleness all became disordered. As he put it: 'Prayer is the graceful flower of gentleness and meekness'.[17] Evagrios counselled that those given to anger can direct it, at the beginning of prayer, to the forces in them and outside them that are rebellious to God,[18] and so expend it in a proper direction before prayer begins. The soul, divided into two parts, that is the energy that desires and the energy that is dynamically aggressive (the concupiscible part and the irascible part in ancient psychological terms), has greater difficulty in controlling its irascible tendencies:

> Whoever controls the powers of anger will have mastery over the demons. But anyone who is a slave to anger will be a stranger to the monastic life, a stranger to the ways of Our Saviour, for as David says: He will teach the gentle his ways. (Ps. 25:9) . . . There is hardly any other virtue which the demons fear more than gentleness . . . which is why the Saviour told us to imitate him in gentleness when he said: 'Learn of me for I am gentle and humble of heart, and there you will find rest for your souls.' (Mt. 11:29). A monk can fast from food and drink, but if he is roused to anger from evil thoughts he will be like a ship sailing the open sea with a demon for a pilot. So keep this watchdog of anger under careful control, training him to destroy only the wolves, not the sheep, and show the greatest gentleness to all who come to you.[19]

THE ASCENT TO PURE PRAYER

Evagrios taught that once a monk had made progress, so that the ordinary run of temptations and distractions had slipped away from his spiritual life, the real battle began. This time, instead of being led astray by the childish level of physical distractions, the soul was pitted against its own natural limitations, what he envisaged as the 'integral movement to desire' which because of the bodily condition makes the balance of spiritual and material in a human being an uneasy and unbalanced relation. The difficulty of guiding a life of prayer then becomes a matter of trying to drive a straight course with an erratic vehicle. The monk's quest for clear self-knowledge at this stage becomes indispensable. Such detailed instructions show Evagrios in his role as an experienced authority trying to provide a psycho-spiritual 'guidance manual' for other monks following the same path of disciplined ascetical prayer. Being able to overcome the soul's tendency to wander in this second stage of development leads to increasing stability and peacefulness in the *nous*. It is this movement which marks the beginning of pure prayer: 'For prayer is the ascent of the spirit before God'.[20] It is at this point that prayer becomes more and more wordless and imageless:

> When the spirit begins to be free of all its distractions as it makes its prayer, then the battle really begins; a day and night struggle against the tendencies of the soul's inner drives. We see a demonstration that passionate disturbance has been transcended when the spirit begins to see its own radiance, when it remains in a state of tranquillity even in the presence of dream images, and when it maintains its calmness even when relating to the affairs of life. A truly healthy spirit is one that at the time of prayer has become free from any images drawn from this world.[21]

The resting in the imageless and wordless state of spiritual *hesychia* is itself the deepest level of invocation that calls down the divine presence:

> So stand guard over your spirit, keeping it free from concepts at the time of prayer. In this way it shall remain in

its own deep calm. Then he who has compassion on the ignorant will come to visit even such an insignificant person as yourself. This is the occasion when you receive the most glorious gift of prayer.[22]

Though Evagrios had much to say about the early stages of praying for his monks, he still believed that 'pure prayer' was the highest and most proper activity of the *nous*. To achieve this advanced state of spiritual consciousness meant 'the putting away of all thoughts'. God is formless and to be united with the true God means to be devoid of all material forms oneself, as far as this was possible in a creature. Pure prayer is to be clearly distinguished from psalmody or other spiritual exercises. Pure prayer means to be imageless, and formless, and enlightened by the grace of the Divine Spirit: the light of the Trinity itself is how he describes it. God, for Evagrios, is not an object of human knowledge but the form of all knowing, and the imageless state of standing in the divine presence is an initiation that is beyond description. If the *Praktikos*, as its name suggests, is concerned with immediately practical issues of ascetic discipline and the psychology of temptation, the 153 *Chapters on Prayer* turn to focus more consciously on the intellective problems to be expected in a life of prayer.

In the *Chapters*, Evagrios defined 'prayer' as the spiritual stasis of the soul conscious of being in the divine presence. All else is preparatory to this:

Prayer is the continual engagement of the spirit with its God. Consider, therefore, that state of soul that will be required to allow a spirit to strain after the Master without vacillation, and live directly and constantly in his presence.[23]

The state of prayer is properly described as a habitual state of dispassion (*apatheia*). It catches up that spirit who loves wisdom in a rapture to the heights of intellective reality, that spirit which is truly spiritualised by the most intense love.[24]

The initiation of prayer, of course, demands the prior efforts at purification. Without this kathartic prelude, prayer does not rise from the ground:

> A man in chains cannot run. A mind that is under the slavery of passions cannot witness the state of spiritual prayer. Such a mind will always be dragged around and violently agitated by these demanding passionate thoughts. It finds it impossible to stand firm in tranquillity.[25]

At the time of prayer itself, the rituals of psychic purification are again necessary as preliminaries. Like Moses, one engaging in prayer lays off the sandals from the feet. These are not just conscious passions, but even every material thought:

> Even Moses was forbidden when he tried to approach the Burning Bush without first removing the sandals from his feet. Just so with you; for you must free yourself from every thought that is coloured by passion, since you desire to see One who is beyond every thought and every perception.[26]

The initial exercise is to pray from the heart, and seek to pray through repentant tears:

> Pray first of all for the gift of tears, for by means of your sorrow you will soften your natural coarseness. Then, having confessed your sins to the Lord, you will obtain pardon for them.[27]

Tears ensure that the 'prayer of the heart' is heard by God, who does not always listen to the careless or the obtuse, despite our often arrogant presumptions that he ought to be always attentive to us whenever we care to address him.

Nevertheless, Evagrios says: 'Pray with tears and your requests will indeed find a hearing.'[28] The door of repentance should then give way to a fixing of the spiritual intellect on the presence of God. This is done by the radical curtailing of the myriad thoughts that begin to rise in the mind:

Stand resolute, and with full attention on your prayer. Pay no heed to the concerns and thoughts that start to arise, for they can do nothing better than disturb or upset you, to the end of dissipating your fixity of purpose in prayer.[29]

Struggle to make your mind deaf and dumb at the time of prayer; for only then will you be able to pray.[30]

It is this brightly focused concentration that, for Evagrios, marks out the person who really prays:

If your spirit is still wandering around at the time of prayer, then it is not yet praying like a monk. You are no better than a man of the world engaged in some kind of dilettante weeding of the garden.[31]

Prayers of petition have their place for Evagrios, but he wryly commented on how it is better to pray to be conformed to the will of God:

Many times when I was at prayer, I would keep on asking for things that seemed good to my understanding. I kept pressing my requests, putting an unreasonable pressure on the will of God. I would not leave it up to his providence to arrange what he knew would be for my best profit. In the end, when I had finally obtained what I asked for, I became very downhearted, at having been so stubborn, for what I received turned out very different in the end from what I had imagined it would be.[32]

When God saw that a soul was making an effort from the heart, Evagrios taught he frequently visited the human spirit with the gift of pure prayer:

The Holy Spirit takes compassion on our weakness, and even though we are far from pure he often comes to visit us. If he should find our spirit praying to him out of love for the truth, he then descends over it and dissipates the whole myriad of thoughts and reasonings that besiege it.

And then he urges it on to the loving desire for spiritual prayer.[33]

For Evagrios, this ascent into the practice of pure prayer effected the metastasis of the spirit, away from the binding world of sensible realities, into the domain of intelligibles. Its psychic faculties now freely move in their proper domain once again, and the human spirit is taught by the angels, whose companion it becomes once more:

> If you pray in truth, you will enter into a deep state of confidence. Then the angels will walk with you and enlighten you concerning the meaning of created realities. Be aware that the angels are urging us on to pray. They stand among us in great rejoicing as they themselves pray for us. Do not provoke them to anger by carelessly admitting distracting thoughts to your prayer.[34]

The angels induct the spirit who has entered into pure prayer into the state of mystical stasis where God will initiate the believer:

> When the Angel of the Lord comes to visit us he dispels by his simple word every conflicting force that operates within us, and he makes it so that the light of our spirits can function clearly. That text in the Apocalypse which refers to the angel who is in charge of putting incense in the bowl containing the prayers of the saints refers, in my opinion, to this particular grace which the angel confers on us, for he infuses into our souls the knowledge of true prayer, and the result is that our spirits can stand firm, for the future, released from the forces of despondency and negligence.[35]

What that initiation of the perfect is, Evagrios will not say. Wordless and imageless, it lies outside the capacity of speech or writing to discuss it. He also deliberately refuses to offer any further 'public' advice for anyone who has arrived at such a state of spiritual practice and experience. His own immediate

context of a close circle of disciples who attended him personally for spiritual counsel explains this discretion. The higher
mysteries of the life of prayer are 'like the soaring aloft of
young eagles',[36] a thing of such perfect beauty and freedom
that it should not be spoken of casually. As he put it in the *Ad
Monachos*:

> Thus honour the Lord and you will know the reasons of
> the Incorporeals; serve him and he will unveil before you
> the systems of the aeons.[37]

One of Evagrios' most appealing works on prayer survived
his sixth-century condemnation because it had already been
translated into Syriac, and was thus out of the reach of the
censorious hands of the Byzantine authorities. It was the
Admonition on Prayer.[38] Here Evagrios is at his most practical
yet most lyrical on the subject of the spiritual life:

> All those who wish to embark on the toils of the virtuous
> life should train themselves to the task gradually, and
> keep on until perfection is achieved. Do not be confused
> by the many different paths our forefathers exemplified,
> and do not try to copy all of them exactly, for this would
> upset your way of life. No, you must choose a way of life
> that suits your lesser abilities. Travel your road and you
> will find life there, for your Lord is merciful, and he will
> find you acceptable not because of your achievements, but
> because of your heart's intention, just as he received the
> poor widow's gift (Mk. 12:43).
>
> Set as your first foundation the spirit of humility. Give an
> example of this foundation in all your gracious words.
> When you worship bend to the ground, and let your con-
> versation be lowly, for in this way you will be loved by
> God and your neighbours.
>
> Allow the Spirit of God to dwell within you. Then, in his
> love, he will come and make a habitation with you. He

will reside in you and live in you. If your heart is pure
you will see him, and he will sow within your heart the
good seed of contemplation upon all his workings, and of
wonder in the face of his glory. All this will come about if
you only take the trouble to weed the garden of your soul
and root out the undergrowth, the brambles and weeds of
your evil desires.

Do not be lax and inattentive in prayer, for you will insult
the Lord who is our Judge. Little person that you are, you
must rouse yourself to prayer and do not wander off. God's
angels are standing around you, do not be afraid. The
hosts of demons are watching opposite you, do not grow
careless.

Such was Evagrios the teacher of prayer. Many of the most
important of the later writers on the patterns of mystical
prayer and spiritual life were ever afterwards in his debt
(whether they acknowledged it or not). His writings greatly
influenced John Cassian who took his doctrine to the western
monks, and they formed a foundational basis for John Climakos and other desert fathers in the Greek East. In the
Orient, spiritual masters such as Isaac of Nineveh spread his
doctrine through the missionary endeavours of the Chaldaean
Church to the far borders of China, and the same was true
in the Christian South, for the Alexandrian Church and the
Ethiopians of the distant highlands studied the substance of
his teachings for centuries in their monasteries. Among the
later Byzantine scholars and theologians, Maximos the Confessor was most heavily indebted to him. In terms of his
originality and his historical impact Evagrios certainly has the
right to be considered one of the major founding fathers of
Christian mystical writing.

4. THE PRAYER OF THE HEART IN THE DESERT TRADITION

THE DESERT AS FERTILE MEETING GROUND

The desert monasteries, particularly those of Syria, Palestine, and Egypt, were powerhouses of Byzantine theology and spiritual writing, and great centres of exchange and debate. In these monasteries the traditions and developments of all three ecclesiastical centres that were their matrix, were processed and adopted as a synthesis that was to have a marked effect on, and wide dissemination through, Byzantium. One might not immediately consider desert monks in the role of disseminators, but it is important to remember also how extensively monastics travelled in Byzantine times, and the religious life of the monks was something that was certainly not restricted to the desert, but always had a large impact on the great Christian cities such as Constantinople, Rome, Antioch, and Alexandria.

The desert communities of Egypt, in particular, played an important synthesising role in regard to spiritual doctrine in the fourth and fifth centuries. Syrian traditions of prayer were already being propagated in the Greek language, and Greek theology of the Origenian tradition was in constant dialogue with them. Both Syrian and Origenian Christian thought came into close proximity in Egypt with local African patterns of spirituality. The resultant mix was potent, and characterised a richly polychromatic spiritual doctrine after the late fourth century which Byzantium adopted and exported to the wider Christian world.

In this present chapter I wish to consider some of the representative voices of the Christian desert. Makarios (an otherwise unknown Syrian writer) can stand as the main voice of the Oriental tradition, though there were numerous others such as Ephrem, or Mar Isaac of Niniveh, who would also deserve an account in a longer study. Evagrios, whom we have already considered, is a typical example of the high Origenistic (Noetic) strand that continued, though much diluted, in most of the important desert communities. Other Greek writers such as Diadochos of Photike, or Dorotheos of Gaza, earned fame as the synthesists of the traditions of the older desert hermits[1] and the new schools of philosophical theologians. This was the generation that first began to issue manuals of spiritual guidance. One of the most famous of these was to be produced by the Abbot of Sinai, John Klimakos.

Makarios, who is really an anonymous fourth-century teacher, represents an important synthesising stage in the literary transmission of the spiritual writings, in so far as his tradition of the Prayer of the Heart soon allied itself to the simpler and concrete apophthegmatic teachings of the Egyptian hermits from the fourth century onwards, making the resultant synthesis the bedrock of most later Byzantine mystical teaching on prayer. Makarios is an unknown, undoubtedly a Syrian, but his influence was so great that his anonymous works were literarily subsumed into the Egyptian tradition by being 'editorially assigned' to the Egyptian ascetic Makarios of Alexandria. The latter was one of the famous 'old men' of the desert who had not left a substantial body of written doctrine of his own, and was thus a prime candidate for being 'taken over' pseudepigraphically. This adoption of Syrian themes from Makarios led to a newly powerful synthesis, a Syro-Egyptian 'tradition of the heart' which in turn set a subtle, and important, difference of tone, in comparison to the previous Evagrian tradition of the human *nous* as the place of encounter with the Godhead.

Often commentators have described the whole generic flow and interpenetration of the Byzantine spiritual schools as a perennial oscillation between the two dominant themes of heart-centred spirituality, and Noetic mysticism. While this is an oversimplification that does not take into consideration exactly how much interconnectedness there is between the two, it is a useful point of consideration that helps distinguish the specific character of the Egyptian and Syrian roots of Byzantine tradition, compared to the more intellectualist Alexandrian–Greek traditions that formed the matrix of theological reflection.

The so-called 'Noetic tradition' of Origen, Evagrios, and Dionysios the (Ps.) Areopagite, never displaced (or even contradicted) the more biblical conception of the attentiveness of the heart as found in the Syrian and Egyptian teachers. Both images, that of the Noetic ascent, and that of the heart becoming aware of the Presence, are drawn from the deep wells of biblical doctrine on the gracious epiphany of the Lord to creatures, and were ultimately to become permanently merged and transmitted in the late Byzantine synthesis of the ascetical tradition that occurred after the tenth century, in Symeon the New Theologian (whom we shall discuss in the later chapter dedicated to Hesychast thought). It is a synthesis, however, that can already be seen to be more or less operative in the fifth- and sixth-century Byzantine spiritual writers.

In so far as we have already spoken earlier about the Evagrian Noetic school of spiritual writing, we need to make an important excursus here, and preface our study of the desert literature by first considering the generic concept of the 'heart' in Christian spiritual theory.

THE HEART IN BIBLICAL AND PATRISTIC THOUGHT

The idea of the heart as the centre of human spiritual awareness of God, and the arena of a disciple's obedience, a dynamic and apocalyptic arena of choice, is a notion rooted in the New Testament, and growing out of the soil of prophetic literature. Paul speaks of the heart as a cipher of the 'innermost self' which longs for the salvation of God (Rom. 7:22). And the

Gospels speak of the heart often as the seat in a human being of understanding and reflection.[2] This is the source of the ancient Christian understanding of the heart as the inner sanctum, where God makes his presence known and commands worship and obedience. Paul summed it up in a famous phrase: 'May your hidden self grow strong, so that Christ may dwell in your heart by faith' (Eph. 3:17). But the most luminous evocation of all the New Testament theology of the heart is the word of Jesus himself in the Beatitudes when he said: 'Blessed are the pure in heart, for they shall see God' (Matt. 5:8). Vision is not a heavily used category in early Christianity for evoking the encounter of the creature with God, but often, as here, when it is used, it is a vision of the heart that is conceived of as having primacy over any vision of the external senses.

When we see the idea of the heart taking a strong and direct role in the writings of the early Eastern Church, therefore, it is primarily as a direct continuance of the biblical tradition that we ought to contextualise it. The sense, as is clearly the case in the Scripture itself, is not so much that it is necessary to seek the heart (as if it were a complex task of spiritual discernment) rather that the heart restlessly, and almost instinctively, seeks after God. A significant aspect of the biblical, and patristic doctrine, however, is that the heart is not alone in its seeking, or even taking the initiative; for God has elected the human heart as the preferred holy ground of the encounter. As with Christ, the Logos incarnate, so now in the spiritual life of the disciple, the heart is destined to become the new Temple of an indwelling holy presence. The heart is not a part of the human creature in the biblical understanding, but connotes the whole creature understood as having a capacity for a higher life, and ultimately a capacity for God who has given his Church the instinct for his presence. The heart, therefore, is the person understood as a creature under the eye of God, a mysterious and holy reality even though creaturely and limited.

As a spiritual arena of encounter, the idea of the heart is

often described in geographical terms in the patristic writings. The terrain of the heart is stark and apocalyptical, like the desert. It is either the holy ground of fiery revelation, or the desolate wasteland of the creature's rebellious and isolated sterility. Prayer, itself a reflection of the condition of this inner heart, retains this apocalyptic character of judgement, that we find especially in the Gospel sayings about the human heart. It is not, in the first instance, an emotional or comfort-laden cipher, in much the way it is used in modern language of spirituality. What this doctrine of the heart essentially says, is that the character of our prayer, like it or not, is a profound indicator of the quality of our true discipleship. This graphic, monistic, and dynamic understanding of the human being in the face of God remains at the core of all the subsequent East Christian understandings of prayer and the spiritual life.

Let us consider now how this generic doctrine of the *nous* and the heart was applied by the various spiritual masters, from the earliest desert abbas to John Klimakos, Diadochos, Makarios and Dorotheos, who shall serve as our representatives of a larger tradition.

THE CHRISTIAN TEACHERS OF THE DESERT TRADITION

The Early Abbas

Monasticism took a strong hold of the spiritual traditions of the Eastern Church, and from the fourth century the desert places adjacent to the Nile, in Egypt, were famed for their monastic communities, and their spiritual elders, or abbas. Some of the most notable among them teach a doctrine of the Prayer of the Heart that was to have an abiding influence on the Byzantine Church's spirituality.

The focus in the earliest levels of the monastic desert teachers is on the necessity for purity of heart. This tradition is summed up in the so-called *Apophthegmata*, the short pithy sayings associated with the early Egyptian ascetics. The tenor of the teachings is concerned with preserving or guarding purity of heart as an absolutely necessary preliminary of true prayer. This is known in Greek as the 'Niptic' tradition. It comes across in two major forms: first (and most commonly) the monk must guard the heart from the stream of defiling thoughts that constantly seem to arise in a human consciousness when it tries to become focused on spiritual realities; and second (in a few of the desert masters) the heart once purified becomes an altar of the radiant presence of God. Antony the Great, cited in the 'The Sayings of the Elders', sums it up as follows:

> A man once said: What good work shall I do?
> And the Abba Antony answered: All works are not equal. The scripture says that Abraham was hospitable, and God was with him; and that Elias loved quiet, and God was with him; and that David was humble, and God was with him. So, what path you find your soul longs after in the following of God, do that, but carefully keep your heart.[3]

Throughout the desert literature the great theme keeps recurring: only in a purified heart can the great mysteries of God be revealed.

Antony's great disciple Ammonas put it like this:

> Night and day I pray that the power of God may increase in you, and reveal to you the great mysteries of the Godhead, which it is not easy for me to utter with the tongue, because they are great and are not of this world, and are not revealed save only to those who have purified their hearts from every defilement.[4]

The Niptic tradition, always conscious of the need for spiritual purity when approaching the Godhead, remained as a constant element in all desert literature, and in the most famous sources, such as the *Apophthegmata*, or the *Lives of the Desert Fathers*, the stress is perennially on the monks as examples of ascetical endurance. Only on rare occasions does one find considered advice on the inner paths of prayer. It is presumed, but is not the central focus of this kind of literature.

John Klimakos

The predominant Niptic literature, however, was not the only textual tradition the desert produced. The manual for monks which John Klimakos, Abbot of Sinai monastery, wrote (*The Ladder of Divine Ascent*), shows the final stage where the desert tradition has moved from purely Niptic writing, advice to beginners and encouragement of asceticism, to the concern to provide a more systematic guidance in the paths of higher psychic awareness. John, who lived from *c.* 579–649, compiled his *Ladder* as a synopsis of the desert monastic tradition. It is still used in the Eastern Church as the guidebook for monastics.

The book is designed in thirty sections, or ladder steps. The first twenty-three explain the vices that are dangerous for monks, and chapters 24-30 interpret the virtues that ought to mark out a progressing disciple. John compares his writing structure to the thirty steps of Jacob's Ladder by which the angels of God ascended and descended over Bethel. It was a particularly apposite simile, as the monastic life was regarded as the life of an earthly angel. Here the traditional Niptic doctrine is combined with much profound material on the higher life of prayer. John had spent many years in strict solitary seclusion, and was famed for his gift of 'unceasing prayer', before he wrote down his instructions as an old man. His teachings followed the pithy apophthegmatic form of the sayings of elders:

> If war demonstrates the soldier's loyalty to the emperor, then prayer demonstrates the monk's love for his God. Your prayer demonstrates exactly what condition you are in. Theologians say that prayer is the mirror of a monk.[5]

> If, while you are praying, you feel inwardly moved, a certain joy, at some word or other, then dwell on it longer. It is a sign that our angel is then praying with us.[6]

When you come to stand before the Lord, let the garment of your soul be woven from top to bottom with the thread of forgetfulness of all those wrongs done against you. Otherwise, your prayer will do you no good at all. Let your prayer be completely simple. Both the Tax Collector and the Prodigal Son were reconciled to God by a single phrase.[7]

As the original settlements of monks soon produced a body of dependencies, with spiritual masters passing on accumulated bodies of wisdom (and literature) to their successors, the greater houses, such as Sinai, or Raithu on the Red Sea, or the hermitages of Skete, began the slow process of accumulating a body of literature intended for the instruction of more advanced monks in the higher mysteries of prayer: those ascetics who had advanced beyond the stage of the pithy short 'sentences' designed for the guidance of beginner monks. It is at this time that individual desert masters began to produce treatises specifically on interior prayer. Evagrios had been one of the first but there were others whose doctrine of the Prayer of the Heart was more concerned with the problem of synthesising together all the varied themes of 'desert spirituality'. Diadochos, Dorotheos, and Makarios are among the greatest of these synthesists who will command our attention next.

Diadochos Bishop of Photike

Diadochos was born *circa* 400 and died sometime before 486 as Bishop of Photike, in Epirus in Northern Greece. Hardly anything is known of his life, but his doctrine on prayer shows that he had close contact with the desert tradition, and wanted to make certain corrections to what he saw as the excessive 'intellectualism' of the Evagrian tradition, which he had read carefully. He does this most notably by giving a theological primacy to love which Evagrios rarely arrives at explicitly. In the process of this realignment he made corrections to the chief terms describing the traditions he received, equating the Evagrian notion of Noetic interiority, with the more biblically grounded conception of the heart. In Diadochos the heart (*kardia*) and the spiritual intelligence (*nous*) have merged semantically. The intellect is the organ of attentive perception, the heart is the locus of the inner self where the meeting with God takes place.

Diadochos was also aware of certain mystical currents then operative, which underestimated the need for bodily involvement in the path of spiritual and psychic development. To offset this gnosticising tendency in Christianity, he emphasises the importance of sacramental life in the Church, and equally stresses the fundamentally 'embodied' character of true prayer. This was why he was a strong advocate of the Jesus Prayer:[8] the necessity for the body to be engaged in the physical confession of the holy name, while the mind worshipped the invisible Godhead. His influence was felt subsequently all through the Byzantine Church.

Against growing tendencies in the Christianity of his time, that focused on the inner human psyche as something deeply corrupted, Diadochos gave a robust defence of the principle of the heart as essentially the graced locus of the encounter with God. It is not the heart which is corrupt, he teaches, but the thoughts of the intellect which we feel in the heart once we have admitted them from outside. His defence of the essential sacramental nature and goodness of the heart rescued the whole Christian doctrine of prayer that was in danger of being destructively radicalised by pessimistic teachings about the inescapability of evil in the human psyche:

> It is true that the heart produces good and bad thoughts from itself (Lk. 6:45) but it does this not because it is the heart's nature to produce evil ideas, but because of the result of the primal deception, the remembrance of evil has, as it were, become like a habit. The heart conceives most of its evil thoughts as a result of the attacks of the demons. But we feel that these evil thoughts arise from

the heart itself, and for this reason some people have inferred that sin dwells in the intellect along with grace; this is because they have little understanding.[9]

Diadochos goes on to affirm the necessity of experiencing directly the workings of God in the inner psychic depths. He locates the arena of the direct sensation of God firmly within the heart, and advances the spiritual taxonomy of the heart by defining it as the seat of spiritual perception, with an inner fixity that is given by its turning to the Lord, and an outer set of attributes which are more open to external sensations and related more closely to the passions. The heart of one who has become fixed on the Lord cannot easily be turned away:

> The reason why we have both good and wicked thoughts together is not, as some suppose, because the Holy Spirit and the devil dwell together in our intellect, but because we have not yet consciously experienced the goodness of the Lord. As I have said before, grace at first conceals its presence in those who have been baptised, waiting to see which way the soul inclines. But when the whole person has turned towards the Lord, then grace reveals to the heart its presence there with a feeling which words cannot express; once again waiting to see which way the soul inclines ... It allows the arrows of the devil to wound the soul at the most inward point of its sensitivity so as to make the soul search out God with warmer resolve and more humble disposition. If, then, a person begins to make progress in keeping the commandments and calls unceasingly upon the Lord Jesus, then the fire of God's grace spreads even to the heart's more outward organs of perception.[10]

Diadochos is anxious to preserve the patristic theology of the heart as the locus of the divine image. Since it is itself in the image and likeness of God, interior observation of the heart is the first step of a divine encounter. He tells how the fall had darkened the inner mirror:

Thereafter it became hard for the human intellect to remember God or his commands. We should, therefore, always be looking into the depths of our heart, with continual remembrance of God, and should pass through this deceitful life like people who have lost their (outward) sight ... The person who dwells continually within the heart is detached from the attractions of this world, and such a person lives in the Spirit and cannot know the desires of the flesh.[11]

For him, the heart is a source of the knowledge of God, which needs attentive introspection to cause the spring to flow out, despite the passions that tend to distract it:

Whenever we fervently remember God we feel the divine longing well up within us, from the very depths of the heart.[12]

This flowing of the grace of the Presence is the work of the Lord from start to end:

The communion of the Holy Spirit brings this about within us, for unless his divinity actively illuminates the inner shrine of our heart, we shall not be able to taste God's goodness with the perceptive faculty undivided.[13]

His doctrine, therefore, is that the ascetic must seek to dwell within this sacred shrine, or temple, of the heart, focusing the attentiveness like a worshipper waiting for the epiphany of the Lord, and using the invocation of the holy name of Jesus to achieve this, until the light of God's revelation breaks forth. Diadochos is not here teaching the later Hesychast or Palamite doctrine, but he is close to it. He is teaching that the light, which is sometimes revealed to the attentive heart, is its own luminosity: but it is a luminosity it possesses exactly in so far as it is the renewed and cleansed Ikon of the True Image who is the Logos, the Archetypal-Creator of the soul:

It is written that none can say Jesus is Lord except in the Holy Spirit (1 Cor. 12:3). Let the spiritual intellect thus continually concentrate on these words within its inner shrine, with such intensity that it is not turned aside to any mental images. Those who meditate unceasingly upon this glorious and holy name in the depths of their heart, can sometimes see the light of their own intellect. For when the mind is closely concentrated upon this name, then we grow fully conscious that the Name is burning off all the filth that covers the surface of the soul.[14]

Diadochos' concern to rebuff a growing Christian pessimism over the fallibility of human motivation, which he noticed in some teachers, sharpened his doctrine of prayer considerably, and changed the character of his writing in the manner of a more coherent taxonomy of prayer. That pessimistic edge Diadochos had noticed, which was wary of the motives of the heart and sought to control the movements of the heart by a refinement of spiritual conscience, was something that was particularly noticeable in the writings of the great Syrian teacher Makarios. It is to this Syro-Byzantine tradition that we shall now turn.

Makarios the Great

Some time in the late fourth and early fifth centuries, a great teacher of the spiritual life was active on the borders between Antioch and the churches of eastern Anatolia. He composed in Greek, and was connected in some way with the Cappadocian circle of monastics. St Gregory of Nyssa knew and used his writing. His real name and history are unknown, but the works which were edited for wider circulation in later times were attributed to the Egyptian desert teacher Abba Makarios, and this was how a Syrian tradition was absorbed into Byzantium via Egypt. Because of the pseudonymous way the teachings were preserved (a sign that some measure of controversy attended the original publication) he is often called Pseudo-Makarios in some modern texts.

Makarios was one of those whom Diadochos opposed

(possibly the main theologian after Evagrios that he wanted to amend), since he believed the spirit of evil was deeply rooted in the human heart, indwelling there like a serpent coiled around the inmost self. Even so, such a doctrine, for Makarios, is not so much a metaphysical dualism, as the root motive for his urging of constant askesis, constant vigilance in the heart, to uproot the incessant promptings of the malign spirits that 'prowl around seeking to devour us' (1 Pet. 5:8). He wishes his disciples (presumably all his immediate monastic following) to apply this psychic awareness to the cause of attuning their life to the spiritual urgings of God's Spirit within the heart:

> What injures and corrupts a person is from within. Out of the heart proceed evil thoughts, as the Lord said (Mt. 15:19) since the things that corrupt a person are within. So, from within is the spirit of evil, creeping and progressing in the soul. It appeals to reason. It incites. It is as the veil of darkness, the 'old man' (2 Cor. 5:17) whom those who have recourse to God must put off, to don the heavenly and new man that is Christ (Eph. 4:22; Col. 3:8). So, nothing of the things that are outside can harm a person except the spirit of darkness that dwells in the heart, alive and active. Each person, then, in their thoughts, must engage in the struggle so that Christ may shine in the heart. To Him be glory for ever.[15]

For Makarios, the landscape of the heart is an apocalyptic arena:

> The heart itself is but a small vessel, yet dragons are there, and there are also lions; there are poisonous beasts and all the treasures of evil. There are rough and uneven roads; there are precipices; but there too is God, the angels, life and the Kingdom, light and the apostles, the heavenly cities and treasures of grace. All things are within it.[16]

In this forty-third *Homily* Makarios gives a taxonomy of the heart in regard to its spiritual condition. His theology, despite the constant stress that the heart is prey to demonic influence, remains optimistic and in accord with the main patristic tradition of the inner image of God within humanity. Christ, he says, has illuminated the human heart like a torch, and in the communion of his light the nature of the Church as a sacrament of Christ is revealed:

> As many torches and burning lamps are lit from a fire, though the lamps and torches are lit and shine from one nature, so too is it that Christians are enkindled and shine from one nature; the divine fire, the Son of God, and they have their lamps burning in their hearts, and they shine before Him while they live on earth, just as He did. This is what it means when it says: So God has anointed you with the oil of gladness (Ps. 45:7).[17]

As the Spirit of God illumined Christ's humanity, and set his heart on fire, so too it is with the true disciple, or the spiritual life counts for nothing:

> If the lamp of a Christian is not enkindled from the light of the Godhead within them, then they are nothing. The Lord was that 'burning lamp' (Jn. 5:35) by means of the Spirit of the Godhead which dwelt substantially in Him, and set his heart on fire, according to the humanity. Consider this image: a dirty old pouch filled with pearls inside. So too Christians in the exterior person ought to be humble and of lowly esteem while, interiorly, in the inner self, they possess the 'pearl of great price' (Mt. 13:46).[18]

For Makarios the enkindling is produced by the heart's constant attentiveness, the watchfulness over the place of the treasure as Christ taught:

> A Christian should always bear the remembrance of God. For it is written: You shall love the Lord your God with all your heart (Dt. 6:5). The Christian should love the Lord, not only when entering into the place of prayer, but also should remember Him in walking, and talking, and

eating, and should love Him in a heartfelt manner. For it says: Where your heart is, there also is your treasure (Mt. 6:21; Lk. 12:34). For to whatever thing a person's heart is tied, or to whichever place a person's desire draws them, this is their god. If the heart always desires God, then God is Lord of our heart.[19]

Makarios constantly urges vigilance. This, he says, is the hard task, the 'working of the earth of the heart'. Vigilance is required for the heart is like an orchard which is bordered by a river whose waters can wash away the foundations if care is not taken. This is why he advocates the practice of 'constant prayer'. The demonic forces that can corrupt the inner self will have no force over a disciple whose heart is founded in the grace of the indwelling Spirit, for constant prayer burns them up like wax in a fire,[20] but should carelessness leave the heart unguarded, spiritual disasters occur:

> Take the example of a garden having fruit-bearing trees and other sweet-scented plants in which all is beautifully laid out. It also has a small wall before a ditch to protect it . . . But should a fast-flowing river pass that way, even if only a little of the water dashes against the wall, it tears away the foundation . . . it enters and . . . destroys the entire cultivation. So it is with the heart of a person. It has the good thoughts but the rivers of evil are always flowing near the heart, seeking to bring it down.[21]

Makarios seems to envisage the constant warfare giving way to progressive stages of stability: at first the heart is constantly hostage to evil thoughts and influences within it, but then its turning to the Lord and its advances in the spiritual life make the presence of the divine Spirit more and more perceptible to the Christian. This growing purity of the heart invites Christ to take up his dwelling within, like a King establishing his Kingdom.[22] In this, Makarios approaches the Evagrian sense of *apatheia*, but in the process makes a radical correction, and displaces the concept of the ascending *nous*, detached

from material attachments, by his more embracing doctrine of
the heart. In Makarios it is the heart which is the seat of the
nous and which encompasses and contains it as the centre of
spiritual awareness: 'There, in the heart, the mind dwells, as
well as all the thoughts of the soul, and all its hopes.'[23]

It was in this aspect of his doctrine, the sense of God's
movement to take command of the heart, that Makarios was
to have his greatest influence over the later Byzantine teachers
of the early Hesychast period. When combined with Diadochos'
suggestion that the purified heart can sometimes see its own
spiritual luminosity, and the Syrian fathers' stress on the
purity of heart that leads to divine theophany, all the materials
for the later Hesychast doctrine of prayer (and the distinctive
theology) are in place, waiting for their resolution.

Dorotheos the Archimandrite[24] of Gaza

Another great synthesist of the Egyptian desert, Dorotheos,
the abbot of the Gaza monastery, was writing at a time in the
sixth century when he suspected the glory days of Christian
Egypt were drawing to a close. He was right. The Islamic
invasions of the seventh century would bring Christianity and
the monastic culture of Egypt to its knees in his land. It
would be a collapse from which it would never recover. We
are fortunate that in his works he writes as if recording and
preserving a great heritage for future use.

Dorotheos represents the doctrine of the heart most particularly. He had been born in Antioch of Syria around 506 and
came to the Egyptian desert in his mid-twenties to learn about
the inner life in the monasteries there. He was one of the most
important of the circle of disciples of Barsanuphios and John,
the two most respected desert teachers of his age. In 540 he
founded his own monastery near the town of Gaza, and for the
brethren he composed a series of *Discourses*. He died at his
monastery sometime after 560. Dorotheos set out consciously
to synthesise the teaching traditions of the Cappadocian
Fathers, Evagrios Pontike, and the simpler *Apophthegmata*

of the desert elders, especially those he claimed as his own (Dorotheos describes Barsanuphios and John as the 'last of the great elders' and sees himself as an archival collector, expositor and arranger of a long prior oral tradition). Like Diadochos after him, he was to be an important link in the combining of the Egyptian and Syrian spiritual traditions for later Byzantine monasticism.

With remarkably personal disclosures, Dorotheos speaks of how the heart moves with God. He encourages his disciples by telling them of a lengthy time of spiritual deadness he experienced, which was ended when he could endure no longer: since God never abandons the faithful disciple to a trial that cannot be endured. He describes an epiphany of Christ in terms of an encounter with a mysterious visitor who gave his heart the grace to rise from its heaviness into joy:

My heart was heavy, my mind was dark, nothing could comfort me and there was no relief anywhere . . . The grace of God comes swiftly to the soul when endurance is no longer possible. Suddenly I turned towards the Church and saw someone who looked like a bishop entering into the sanctuary . . . Something drew me powerfully after him, so I went into the Church behind him. He remained standing for some time with his hands stretched up to heaven, and I stood there in great fear, praying, for I was very alarmed by the sight of him. When his prayer was finished he turned and came towards me, and as he drew nearer to me I felt my pain and dread passing away. Then he stood in front of me and, stretching out his hand, touched me on the breast and tapped my chest with his fingers saying the words of the psalm: I waited. I waited on the Lord and he stooped down to me; he heard my cry. He drew me from the deadly pit, from the miry clay. He set my feet upon a rock and made my footsteps firm. He put a new song into my mouth – praise of our God. (Ps. 40:1–2). He repeated all these verses three times, tapping me on the chest as I have said. Then he departed.

> And immediately light flooded my mind and there was joy
> in my heart, with comfort and sweetness. I was a different
> man. I ran out after him hoping to find him but I could
> not. He had vanished. From that moment on by God's
> providence, I have not known myself to be troubled by
> fear or sorrow, for the Lord has sheltered me up till this
> moment through the prayers of the old men.[25]

For Dorotheos, the heart is all that matters in the movement
of the spiritual life. If it is ready, then its eagerness ensures
the presence of God:

> If anyone really and truly desires to do the will of God with
> all their heart, God will never leave them to themselves,
> but will constantly guide them according to His own divine
> will. If someone really sets their heart on the will of God,
> God will enlighten a little child to tell such a person what
> is His will. But if a person does not truly desire the will
> of God, even if they were to go to search out a prophet,
> God would put into the mouth of that prophet a deception
> similar to that which was in that man's own deceiving
> heart.[26]

His 'spiritual maxims' show a character who, for all his
mystical flights, was grounded deeply in ordinary communal
life:

> Do not look for the love of those of your company. If you
> look for love, and the other does not respond in like
> manner, how you will be troubled. Instead, determine only
> to show your own love for your neighbour, and then you
> will find rest for your heart, and by this means you will
> also lead your neighbour to God.[27]

His years of the experience of close living in monastic community made him realise that the immediate community is
the proving ground of our love and our authenticity. Far from
being the greatest hindrance to a perfected Christian life, the

rough fabric of communal existence is the fundamental earth from which the spiritual life grows:

> May our God, who is so good, give us good disposition of heart, that we might gain some benefit from every single person, and never think badly of our neighbour. Even if our own state of mind is such that we do think, or suspect, ill of our neighbour, let us try as quickly as we can to change those thoughts into something kind and beautiful. For if we try never to notice anything bad in our companions, that disposition soon changes, with God's help, into a state of virtue that is truly well-pleasing to God. To Him be glory and honour.
>
> To the Ages of Ages. Amen.[28]

THE PRAXIS OF THE PRAYER OF THE HEART

The desert communities, and the great spiritual teachers that emerged from them, played a very important role in the formulation of a Christian spiritual doctrine that was at once transcendent in its aspirations and still concretely grounded in the realities of human psychology. In this sense the Christian desert proved to be a fertile and active meeting place. Its great achievement can be summed up as defining a new sense of 'the Prayer of the Heart'.

This quintessential East Christian doctrine of the Prayer of the Heart, however, is not comparable (certainly not reducible) to the later western concept of praying with the heart, meaning 'affective prayer', traditionally understood as a lower stage of spiritual development than pure contemplation. The tradition of the 'Prayer of the Heart' stands against such a schema at many key points. Equally, it is necessary to state that neither is it reducible (as is often supposed in many modern Orthodox writings about the Prayer of the Heart) simply to the Jesus Prayer,[29] though the tradition of the Jesus Prayer certainly fits within the overall schema of the 'Prayer of the Heart', where short phrases (praying – *monologistos*) repeated with attentiveness (*prosoche*) provide a method of returning with sober repentance (*penthos*) to the consciousness of the heart and the One who dwells patiently within it, other to us.

All in all, the early Byzantine doctrine of the heart points to a profoundly biblical mystery. The heart has been made as the centre of a creature's being. But it is a creature of God to whom the gift of salvation has been offered, and for whom the potential to engage in communion with the transcendent God is ever a possibility. For this reason the heart is no neutral ground. It is sacred space. It is a place of epiphany. The first epiphany of which the fathers speak is that which occurs in the heart as a creature sees the self revealed, when the turmoil of passionate desires that keep the heart from recognising itself, have been stilled by a necessary purification and *hesychia*. This first revelation that takes place is followed, if such a 'turning of the heart' proves itself as an act of the whole person, a heartfelt act of pure sincerity, by the corresponding movement of God who reveals himself to the heart. The syntax chosen for this in patristic language is frequently that of a luminous encounter, itself a profoundly biblical expression of the divine epiphany.

The most insistent aspect of the doctrine, however, is not so much the light-filled encounter with God – always carefully described as God's approach to the creature, and never the creature's ascent to the divine (in which it emerges as thoroughly Christian in its spiritual instinct) – for this is treated with typical reserve in the patristic texts, and one comes across it obliquely as if a veil is being drawn over such moments, moments that ought not to be talked of before they have been experienced by the hearer directly (*cor ad cor loquitur*[30]); the most insistent aspect of the doctrine, it seems to me, is the teaching that the entire movement of God to the human being is rooted and grounded in the fabric of the whole person, that is body and soul, heart and mind. The heart stands as the central locus of the whole spiritual intelligence, but an awareness that is conditioned by physicality. For the Byzantine teachers, true prayer is not that which escapes this embodiment (an incarnate existence which even the divine Logos did not despise when he made this fragile image take on the potential to contain the uncontainable presence of the Godhead) rather prayer that rises from a penitent heart. True prayer thus offers the penitence of the heart as its first offering: a heart that is conscious of its forgetfulness and error, but one that quickly passes beyond sorrow, through the instinct of the abundant mercy of its Lord, to the confession that ours is a God who wishes to commune with creatures in the depths of a pure heart which has been rendered 'blessed' in Christ and thereby promised the vision of God.

Nowhere better is it summed up than in those words of the Church's first, and greatest, teacher of prayer: 'How blessed are the pure in heart for they shall see God' (Matt. 5:8).

5. GOD'S SINGERS: THE BYZANTINE POETIC TRADITION

THE DEVELOPMENT OF METRICAL THEOLOGY IN BYZANTIUM

The first vehicle of all Christian theology, after the preached sermon, was undoubtedly the song, or hymn. In the East Christian Churches this aspect of theological tradition was centrally important from the earliest times, so much so that hymnal theology is a major and foundational level of New Testament Christological confession. The list of hymns embedded in the Gospels and Letters is impressive, chief among them: the Magnificat (Luke 1:46ff.); the Benedictus (Luke 2:29–32); the Logos Hymn (John 1:1–18); the *Kenosis* Hymn (Phil. 2:5–11); the Hymn to the Cosmic Christ (Col. 1:15–20); the Credal Hymn (1 Tim. 3:16); and the Marriage Song of the Lamb (Rev. 19:1ff.). Along with the Psalms, such hymnic theology was highly formative in the liturgical life of the early Eastern Church. Ambrose of Milan, the father of the Latin Church's hymnic tradition, had already noticed in the fourth century how extensively the theological song was being used in the East Christian world, and successfully emulated the practice, giving birth to a magnificent Latin hymnic tradition after him. In this chapter we will look more particularly at four of the great poets of the Byzantine tradition: Gregory of Nazianzus, Romanos the Melodist, Kassia the Nun, and John of Damascus.

Byzantium was always a great melting pot of Christian cultural traditions. Its chief language was Greek, but its near neighbours were Syrian, and its range of influence spread

as far afield as Ethiopia. Two church traditions particularly
affected the development of the Byzantine Hymn as a theological and spiritual form. The first was the Greek literary
tradition of the theological hymn proper. It had long been
customary in Egyptian and Greek Mystery religion to chant a
theological hymn honouring the Godhead. Some fine poetic
examples still exist, not least the 'Hymn to Amen Ra' from
Egypt, and the Stoic 'Hymn to Zeus' by Cleanthes, or the
'Hymn to Apollo at the feast of Karna'.[1] Most of the surviving
examples from late antiquity are poetic, hieratic, and highly
philosophical in tone. Some of the New Testament hymns,
those which are not more immediately rooted in Old Testament
or Psaltic forms, also belong to this tradition.[2] It was, however,
the Greek theologians of the fourth century who really took the
hymnic theological form to its highest development, and at
the same time gave the Byzantine liturgy its magnificently
poetic and mystical character.

The second development was something that came from the
Syrian Church's preaching tradition. Following ancient semitic
customs, the Syrians from earliest times had developed the
form of the sermon using biblical allusion and cross-reference
to such an extent that the entire homiletic became an extended
biblical commentary. As one can see in the preaching of Jesus
himself, the principle was followed that the only valid commentary on Scripture is Scripture itself. The text that was being
preached on was, therefore, merged with a kaleidoscopic
weave[3] of other texts illuminating it. This tradition, known as
midrashic commentary, led to the practice of proclaiming the
Scriptures aloud with an extended biblical commentary wrap-
ping the central narrative in an indivisible fashion. Soon, this
function of proclaiming the Scriptures was set musically, and
the genre of midrashic hymn was born. The transmittal of this
form to Byzantium, and its translation into Greek gave a
massive stimulus to the development of midrashic scriptural
hymns in the Byzantine Church. Romanos the Singer is one
of the chief examples of this genre. He himself was a Syrian
Christian, working as a hymnographer in the great church of

Hagia Sophia in Byzantium. His various hymns all show how the central biblical narrative being considered is turned over and over again, like a man examining a rare jewel, from every related scriptural angle, so that in the end a veritable 'Persian carpet' of biblicisms emerges in the hymn, to show how the feast that is currently being celebrated in the liturgy is fixed firmly within the greater wall of the biblically recorded events of salvation. One way in which the Byzantine hymn achieves this is the constant appeal to biblical 'types'.[4] Mary's virginal pregnancy, for example, is like the bush at Sinai that was blazing with the presence of the deity, but never consumed by the raging fire; or she is that 'sealed well' which the patriarch spoke of in the ancient history of Israel; or Christ is like Abraham's beloved son carrying the wood of his own sacrifice up the mountain of his immolation.

Typology elides time and space, in the creative act of interpreting the whole history of salvation Christocentrically. The midrashic hymns, the form the Byzantine Church came to adopt most generally, soon spread through the whole liturgical service, providing an endless biblical chant, like a diapasonal bass tone sounding throughout the entire worship. To this day the Byzantine church services are sung, never simply spoken, and the wealth of symbolic imagery provides a dazzling array of icons to the mind and ear, just as the church building provides a large vista of imagery to the eye, assisting the mind and imagination of the worshippers to understand the significance of the events they celebrate, and thereby rise from the historical event to the perennial experience of the salvation it signifies.

ST GREGORY OF NAZIANZUS: THEOLOGIAN AND POET

Gregory of Nazianzus (c. 330–91) was the son of a bishop in Cappadocia, the eastern part of modern Turkey, north-east of Antioch of Syria, and in Christian antiquity known as Galatia. The province had a Christian history reaching back to the apostle Paul, and in the fourth century was a centre for a highly impressive Christian intellectual renaissance, in which Gregory featured prominently. He is known as one of the 'Cappadocian Fathers' in the company of St Basil the Great, and St Gregory of Nyssa. Gregory was one of the chief theologians responsible for the final triumph of the Nicene faith (the doctrine of Jesus' full divinity, fully present in the body) and was also the chief architect of the classical Christian doctrine of the Trinity: three co-equal persons in one single divine nature. His family were immensely wealthy land-owners, and, along with his brother Caesarios, Gregory was given the finest education then available. He spent ten years in Athens learning the craft of rhetoric in speech-making and poetry, and had already determined to dedicate his life to Christ in ascetical seclusion when his father summoned him back to the estates in Cappadocia to assist him in his business there. Gregory's pleading to be allowed to live out a vocation in the monastic life fell on deaf ears, as far as his father was concerned, and since he was the local bishop, there was little that the son could do about it. In line with a custom that was then in force, his father compelled him to be ordained to the priesthood at the town of Nazianzus, and later on St Basil and his father also conspired to have him consecrated a bishop, much against his will. Although he dutifully delivered the sermons in the local church for several years, as priest and suffragan bishop, straight after his father's death he slipped away from Cappadocia to the monastery-shrine of St Thekla in Seleucia. No sooner had he established himself there, however, than he was summoned by a large synod of eastern bishops gathered in Antioch, to spearhead a mission to the imperial city of Constantinople, which was currently held by the Arian clergy who denied the divinity of Christ. He obeyed their call and spent almost two years preaching a series of orations on the catholic faith in the capital. At first he was stoned in the streets for his pains, but soon he became the most celebrated orator in the city, and when the new Emperor Theodosius arrived in 380 to claim his capital, Gregory was appointed the orthodox Archbishop of Constantinople. In this capacity he presided over the ecumenical council held there in 381, after which he retired to live back in seclusion on his estates in Cappadocia, spending his final years editing the most magnificently learned dossier of sermons any Christian since Origen had ever produced. In this Indian summer of his life he composed innumerable poems and hymns, trying to simplify the complexities of Christological and trinitarian dogma for congregational instruction in hymnic form. His principle was always that true theology is only that which is expressed by the Church's deepest instincts when at prayer, and ought to be celebrated in the liturgy. His poems range from small-scale personal pieces, to accounts of mystical vision, and theological catechesis. His writings became the single most copied source in Byzantium after the Bible, and he was soon regarded as the supreme 'patristic' authority, earning the title of 'St Gregory the Theologian'. Many of his poems went on to become standard models for the later Byzantine liturgical poets Romanos, John Damascene and Cosmas the Singer.

Gregory's writings, long unknown in the West, are now beginning to appear for the first time in modern English translations.[5] Gregory understood the whole dynamic of the spiritual life to be a progressive purification of the human being, through prayer and study, until a refinement of mind and soul was achieved that sensitised the Christian to the radiant presence of God and his angels all around. When the soul was sufficiently purified to be aware of the heavenly liturgy surrounding it, it was also, at that same moment, invited to join in the chorus of praise, and to take its rank in the company of the immortal spirits who will comprise the heavenly court of God. His doctrine of angels is very important to his thought. These are the spirits of fire who surround God with constant praise, and who draw their life from the very presence of the deity, in perfect communion of love with God and each other. They offer to the Church and to the individual Christian a model of existence and behaviour. When a saintly life is modelled on them, the true disciple also finds that he or she is rendered into a 'fire of love', a consuming and enveloping fire which is how God wraps the creature into a new and divine destiny. It is almost as if Yeats was thinking of Gregory when he wrote those famous lines of his poem that have been taken as our book's title: 'sages standing in God's holy fire'. The icon of Gregory scintillating in a sea of gold mosaic is one of the standard iconic patterns of most Byzantine churches, and the iconography follows much of Gregory's mystical point in his writings: namely that closer and closer approximation to God in prayer leads to an elevation of the human spirit into a transcendent status, analogous to the angels whose natures are like spiritual fire. Prayer, in short, lifts a human being from earth to heaven even in this lifetime. It marks the advent of God to the soul, and this in and of itself marks the deification of the believer by the very presence of the Lord.

The following example of his poetry shows him ranging from personal prayer of repentance to a cosmic sense of the transcendent glory of God, as chanted by the angels in the heavenly choir. Gregory designates his hymn a 'Thanksgiving'. In Greek the double meaning is more clearly underlined. His poem is a 'Eucharist', and in the course of it the human heart is itself eucharistically transfigured by the divine power:

Hymn of Thanksgiving

All thanks to you, the King of All, and maker of all
    things.
All thanks to you, who by your Word
        commanded spiritual and material forms,
And summoned into being what was not there before,
        from nothingness bringing them forth.
Those perfect singers of your praise
        stand gathered round your throne.
The myriad of angelic ranks, untold myriads yet again,
That fiery chorus all unmarred, since time has first
    begun,
The first-born nation, with a choir of radiant stars,

Those spirits of your righteous saints, the souls of all the
   just,
All are gathered in as one, to stand around your throne,
To make their hymn with ceaseless joy and awe.
They chant a song both endless and sublime:
'All thanks to you, Most Mighty King and maker of all
   things!'
A hymn indeed sublime, that issues from that heavenly
   choir.
And yet, I too shall make my prayer:
Immortal Father, before you I shall bend the knee,
which signifies my heart.
Immortal Father, before you I prostrate my inmost mind.
I rest my brow upon the ground, to make my prayer
   before you,
A suppliant in your sight. I pour out the libation of my
   tears.
How could I be ever worthy of raising my eyes so high
   above?
Merciful Father, take pity on me.
Have mercy on your servant who so implores your grace.
Stretch forth your hand, and cleanse my inmost
   thoughts,
And snatch me then from out the jaws of death.
Never deprive me of your Holy Spirit.
So pour your courage and your strength into this soul of
   mine
That I may ever hymn you with all my heart and voice.[6]

ST ROMANOS THE SINGER

Romanos, one of the greatest of all the Byzantine lyrical poets,
flourished as a deacon in the Great Church at Constantinople
around 540. He was one of the musical directors and composers
of Hagia Sophia in all its glory after Justinian commissioned
the new church. He was born late in the fifth century at Emesa
(Homs), and was thus Syrian by ethnic origin. He belonged to

a Jewish family: but whether he converted or his parents had already become Christians, is unknown. He was first a deacon at Beirut, and thence moved to Constantinople at the end of Emperor Anastasios' reign, settling in the Monastery of the Mother of God in the quiet district of Kyros in the north of the capital city some time around 515. By the time of his death in 555, he had gained an international stature as one of the greatest hymnographers of the Eastern Church.

It is possible that the greatest of all Byzantine Marian hymns, the *Akathistos*,[7] is one of his compositions, but opinion is divided on the issue. A tenth-century *Synaxarion* lists his liturgical feastday as being commemorated on 1 October. The entry shows how his gift was already commonly regarded as miraculous:

> In the monastery church of the Mother of God, the vener-able Romanos received the gift of composing Kontakia, when the Holy Virgin appeared to him in a dream on the vigil of Christ's Nativity, and gave him a scroll which she ordered him to eat. As soon as he had swallowed it he immediately woke from his trance, and climbing the steps of the pulpit began to chant and declaim his hymn – *Today The Virgin*.

Romanos was the leading exponent of the *Kontakion* style of hymnography: the religious sermon chanted to music, that same midrashic tradition rooted in the ancient Syrian custom of metrical sermonising. Eighty 'metrical sermons' have sur-vived under his name, though some are of doubtful attribution. Several of his *Kontakia*, especially the hymns: 'On the Nativity', 'On the Presentation in the Temple', 'On the Resur-rection', and 'The Virgin's Lament at Calvary' are considered masterpieces of world-literature. The following selections will give a brief flavour. When heard chanted by a choir in the ancient, flowing Byzantine melodies, they have a resonant and mystically hypnotic effect that is difficult to imagine merely reading the cold page. The endless roll of melody and the poetic abundance of images piling up association after association, each stressing paradoxical contrast after contrast in the life of Christ, all lead to an overwhelming sense of absorption and initiation into the very events that are being described. The song, in a sense, has designed itself to open up the mystery of Scripture so that the hearer can enter in and participate through a variety of senses, and at a deeper level than the merely intellectual. The 'Christmas Hymn' is presented here in its prelude and first stanzas recounting the story of the birth of Jesus, Mary's inner thoughts, and the visit of the Magi. By the constant reiteration of paradoxes, Romanos draws a scheme of the divine mystery emerging from the poorest signs: the poverty of the birth as a sacrament of the abundant richness of salvation in and through the divine Lord. Mary, as birth-giver of God (*Theotokos*), is also the midwife of the election of the Gentiles:

A Christmas Hymn
This day the Virgin gives birth to One beyond all being.
The Earth offers a cave to the Unapproachable One.
Angels join shepherds in giving glory;
Magi journey with a star;
For, for our sakes, there is born:
A tiny child, who is God before all ages.

Bethlehem has opened Eden's gate.
Come let us see.
A delight has been found, hidden away in secret.
Come let us take the gifts of paradise
From within a cave.

There stands revealed a root that was never watered
    [Isa. 11:1]
Which has blossomed out in forgiveness.
There has been found the Undug Well,
Which, long ago, David longed to drink from [2 Sam.
    23:13–17].
For there a virgin has given birth to a child,

And straightway ended the thirst of Adam and of David.
And so, let us hurry to this place where there has been
   born:
A tiny child, who is God before the ages.

One who was that mother's father,
has elected to become her son.
The Saviour of all children is laid as a child in a manger;
And his mother, comprehending this, spoke thus to him:
Tell me, child, how were you sown?
how were you planted in me?
Seeing you, my own flesh, I stand amazed,
For I give suck but am not married.
I see you before me wrapped in swaddling bands,
Yet still know the flower of my virginity is inviolate.
For so it pleased you to preserve it when you were born:
A tiny child, who is God before the ages.

Most High King, what have you in common with the
   poor?
Why, Maker of the Heavens, have you come to earthly
   kind?
Were you so anxious for a cave? so desirous of a manger?
But see, there is no place for your handmaid at the Inn.
There is no place, I say, not even a cave;
For that too belongs to others.
And yet, when Sarah bore her child,
She was given a great land as her inheritance.
But I have not even a foxes' lair [Matt. 8:20].
I had to use that grotto in which it pleased you to dwell:
A tiny child, who is God before the ages.

As she spoke these words secretly inside herself,
Entreating One who has the knowledge of all secrets,
She heard the Magi arrive, who had come to seek the
   child.
At once the maiden cried: And who are you?

And they replied: But who are you to have born such a
    son?
Who is your father? Who is she who bore you?
That you should become the mother
and nurse of this fatherless son.
For we saw a star, and understood that there has
    appeared:
A tiny child, who is God before the ages . . .

When Mary heard these words so strange,
She bent low and worshipped the child of her own womb,
And weeping, she cried out:
You have done great things for me, my child,
Great are all the things you have done for me
            in my poverty [Luke 1:46–9].
For behold, the Magi are outside,
Kings of the eastern lands, seeking you.
The rich among your people
            petition to have audience before you.
For your people are those to whom you have been made
    known:
A tiny child, who is God before the ages.[8]

The Virgin's Lament

The song of Mary's lament on Calvary is of heart-breaking
intensity. Used in the Passion services it set a tone of mourning
for the burial of Christ that still liturgically marks the Byzantine Holy Week services for Great Friday:

As she saw her own lamb being dragged off to slaughter
    [Isa. 53:7]
The ewe-lamb Mary followed after, worn out,
in the company of the other women, crying out:
Where are you going my child?
For whose benefit do you run this course so quickly?
Is it another wedding, as at Cana?

Is it going there that makes you hurry so
That you can turn their water to wine once more ...?[29]

The song develops by depicting Christ on his way to the cross counselling his mother not to grieve so broken-heartedly, for his eagerness to deliver the world of suffering beings gives him a zeal that few can comprehend. The vinegar will be an astringent which the Physician of life shall use to cure the wounds of humankind. The spear lances humanity's festering wounds; the clothes of Christ bandage the suffering body; the cross serves as a splint and a crutch for the healing of humanity's sicknesses and mortality.

The Victory of the Cross

In his song on the Victory of the Cross, also probably written for Great Friday Services but now used for the feast of the Veneration of the Cross beginning on the Third Sunday of Lent, Romanos uses the graphic image of the roots of the tree of the cross breaking down into the roof of the cavern of hell. The rupture makes the Evil Spirit sick and forces him to disgorge the human race held captive there. A tree and its fruit caused the imprisonment of the whole race in death, and just so, Romanos sings, another Tree has set humanity free to live a greater life. Romanos depicts the Devil crying out to hell personified, 'The eyeless calling out to the sightless', and advising it not to be so weak-spirited. Even if a Cross breaks into hell, Satan argues, nothing is powerful enough to liberate the lost souls or restore them to Paradise. But when Satan hears the words spoken to the thief, 'This day you will be with me in Paradise', his knees give way and he realises that indeed Paradise has once more been laid open. All too late he comprehends the significance of the Cross in all the Old Testament 'types' that have mystically prefigured it. The Cross has become that wooden spar to which the shipwrecked cling, which carries them to safety:

All cling to the Cross as if to the Tree of Life,
cling to it and swim, and so make good their escape
coming home to a safe harbour:
And so once more to Paradise we come.[10]

It was an image Romanos chose carefully, addressing a nation of seafarers in what was then the greatest port of the ancient world. His music and his rolling waves of textual icons all were pressed into the service of a creative and highly coloured retelling of the gospel of salvation.

KASSIA THE POETESS

The nun Kassia is perhaps the most famous of the Byzantine women hymnographers. She lived sometime between 805 and 867. The legend of her life tells that she had been one of the aristocratic Byzantine ladies presented to the Emperor Theophilos as a potential wife, who assumed the religious life after she was passed over as empress, founding a convent in Constantinople, for which she composed her hymns and ethical verse instructions. Letters exist from the great ninth-century saint, Theodore the Studite, which are addressed to his supporter Kassia the nun, and if this is the same as the poet, then she must have been active at a very high level in the Iconoclastic controversy, as a defender of the Icons, and as a monastic reformer alongside St Theodore.

Her most famous single piece is the midrashic reflection on the repentant sinful woman entitled 'To the Harlot'. It is a highly dramatic identification with the sinful woman who weeps over the death of Jesus as she brings myrrh. Kassia invites her singers to enter into the dynamic experience of conversion by identification with the character's dialogue with Christ. It held such a power that it eventually entered into the Triodion, the Byzantine church service book for Lent. The paradoxes that delighted most of the Byzantine poets are much in evidence here. The woman weeps over the dead Christ, but it is the Living Lord with whom she has her conversation. The light has gone from the world, but it is the darkness of her own sins that causes her sorrow. The tears she offers are a small gift to one whose power lets the waters of the oceans drop from the clouds. But they are enough, the signs of a loving heart, to ensure that as he once stooped down from heaven to empty himself out in love in his incarnation, so now he will bend down low again and hear his servant's cry:

> Lord, the woman who fell headlong into a multitude of
>   sins
> still recognised your Godhead,
> and joined the ranks of the Myrrh-bearing women.
> Dropping tears she carries myrrh for you
> before you were laid in the tomb;
> crying out: Alas! what dark night envelops me;
> what gloomy, moonless, madness of abandonment
> is the lust for sin I have.
> But take this offering of my spring of tears,
> you who guide the waters of the seas
> through the paths of clouds.
> Stoop down to me, for the great grief my heart bears;
> you who made the very skies bow down,
> before the face of your ineffable self-emptying.
> How I shall kiss your immaculate feet!
> and once again I shall dry them with the hair of my
>   head;
> those feet whose steps Eve once heard, at dusk in
>   paradise,
> and then hid herself in fear.
> Who can ever sound the depths of my sinfulness
> or the profundities of your judgements,
> O My Saviour, the Deliverer of our souls?
> Do not pass by this your handmaid,
> you who have such boundless mercy.[11]

JOHN OF DAMASCUS

John (*c.* 675–749) is traditionally called the 'Damascene' but his work as a Christian priest-monk and theologian was largely centred around Palestine, particularly the desert monastery of Mar Saba in the Judaean wilderness near Bethlehem. He was a member of an important Christian family in Damascus under the Islamic caliphate, holding the political office of Logothete after his father. His duties involved representing the Christians at the court of the Caliph, policing his minority and oppressed community, and raising taxes from them. His Islamic overlords increasingly came to regard him with suspicion, and in this tense climate he left the city in the early eighth century, and elected to live in the monastery of Mar Saba, a Christian intellectual and cultural oasis in territories that had long belonged to the Byzantine world, but had in recent centuries fallen under Islamic domination. It was this location outside Byzantine imperial control that allowed John to emerge into public fame as a great defender of the theology of Icons. The Byzantine court at this time was mounting a bitterly hostile campaign against sacred images, denouncing them as idolatrous or at best distracting from true Christianity. In the course of this pogrom the authorities were persecuting the monks of the empire who were the defenders of the icons as a traditional part of Christian faith and worship. John, from his vantage point of being outside the reach of the emperor, became the main theological spokesman for the significance of icons, arguing that images had never been forbidden by the Scriptures as such, and it was no good argument to appeal to the Old Testament as proscribing Christian icons. Where images had been forbidden, in the Old Testament, it was because they were used in pagan cult. As well as the prohibition of idolatry, however, the sacred Scripture contained numerous commandments to adorn the ancient Temple with cherubim and other rich imagery, in the service of the worship of the Living God. The same Bible that condemned images of false gods, thus advocated, and even prescribed, the imagery required in the worship of the true God in his earthly shrine.

John's concluding argument in his treatise *Defence of the Holy Icons* was that a tendency to iconoclasm in Christian life and worship represented an excessive Platonism, a belief in the superiority of spiritual affairs over material affairs in the life of Christians. For John, the essence of Christian faith was given in the God-Man Jesus. God was not partially or imperfectly revealed in the incarnation of Christ, John argued, but entirely and fully present. The flesh of the Lord, therefore, was the perfect medium of divine presence and revelation. It stands revealed as the powerful paradigm of how divine grace shall enter in materiality and transfigure it by grace. The icon can thus be a holy thing, just as relics and other particular material forms, like the cross, or holy water, can be sacramental vehicles of grace. This sacramentality does not stop at holy things, however, since all Christians are drawn into this process of incarnational transfiguration in Christ: he who proves that the old dividing lines between Creator and Creature, between spirit and flesh, between God and humankind, have all been elided in the new dispensation of the gospel of the incarnate Lord. In short, the icon, by an extension from the act of incarnation, is comparably a material medium that carries the grace of the figure it depicts (Christ or the Virgin or a saint). It is like a sacrament of the presence of the holy figure it depicts, and calls down a blessing on those who pray by means of it. John's defence of the icons made him one of the most famous of the later 'fathers' of the Eastern Church. He is sometimes called the 'last of the fathers'.

His doctrine on the icons was vindicated at the Seventh Oecumenical Council in 787. His life coincided with the time the Byzantine Church in its political, as well as its cultural and religious life, was entering upon a long and slow plateau. As a theologian John emerges as a synthesist, not as a great innovator. He compiled great collections of patristic writings that were meant to sum up the 'orthodox tradition' as it had been established. His work subsequently had a wide circulation in the East as well as the West, and was the main source for Aquinas' *Summa Theologiae*.

John and his adoptive brother Cosmas gave new life to the Byzantine tradition of hymn writing, and they were ideally situated as Mar Saba monastery had become a great force in the renewal of the eastern liturgy of the hours, that was well under way by the ninth century. John's hymns, as well as those of Cosmas, are found throughout Byzantine church services, and used regularly even to this day.

Some of the feelings of Christians in the Orient, hardpressed by the encroachments of Islam, can be sensed in the imagery of this 'Hymn to the Virgin':

Hymn to the Virgin

Let us sing a hymn to Mary the Virgin,
That heavenly Gate, and glory of our world;
That new bud of humankind that gave birth to the Lord.
Of her the angels make their song,
The proud boast of all the Church,
For she received within herself, no less than heaven,
The very temple of our God.
And she has broken down the dividing-wall of enmity;
Has brought about our peace,
Opened access to the throne of God.
Hold fast to her, the anchor of our faith.
Her we have as mighty champion
Who from her own self gave the Lord of all his birth.
And so, take heart you people of God,
For he himself shall gird for war, against our many foes;
He who is the Lover of Mankind.[12]

In the following short and dense hymn on the triumph of the cross (now used as the central Byzantine hymn for feasts of the cross in the liturgy) John presents the crucifixion as the paschal victory that refigures the entire race in the image of the immortal God. It is a precise encapsulation of the mystical Byzantine understanding of the cross and resurrection as a living mystery of salvation. The redemption is not merely an atonement that leads to humanity's forgiveness, it is even more an ontological change that takes place in the fabric of the disciple's life: the gift of deification by grace:

Hymn to the Life-giving Cross

Ceaselessly we bow, O Christ our God,
Before your Cross that gives us life;
And glorify your Resurrection, Most Powerful Lord,
When on that third day you made anew
The failing nature of Mankind,
Showing us so clearly the way back to heaven above.
For you alone are Good,
The Lover of Mankind.[13]

These few poetic pieces from the tradition can only give a sense of the power of the Byzantine liturgical hymn. When sung in the dark chanting and characteristic 'bending notes' of the Byzantine melodies such high theological text can and often does enter into the fabric of the heart with a peculiar intensity. The sung midrash opens up the eye of the heart to new understandings of the glory of God.

6. SAINTS AND THEIR HAGIOGRAPHIES IN BYZANTIUM

AN ASCETIC CATALOGUE

The great majority of sources that exemplify the Byzantine theological and spiritual tradition are so thoroughly celibate-ascetic and episcopal, composed by monastics and clergy as well as maintained in the literary tradition by them, that it is hardly surprising that either the monastic or the liturgical paradigm is the dominant motif of almost all of the surviving religious writings. This it is which gives Byzantine theology its special ethos, and yet it would be a mistake to see the monastic writings or the high theology of the church 'fathers' as exhaustive of the eastern tradition.

Byzantium was always one of the most cultured and sophisticated centres of Christian experience throughout antiquity, and the role of the laity was always highly important. The role of women in the formation and development of the traditions of Christian spirituality may nowhere be as important in antiquity, after the New Testament period, as in Byzantium, though it is only relatively recently that proper scholarly attention has been given to this aspect of church history, revealing the considerable influence that women exercised in the Eastern Christian Church and empire. As with many other aspects of life in late antiquity and the early Middle Ages, the ancient rhetorical textual tradition did not always recognise or focus on many aspects of reality, even those that were under its nose as important factors. There are, for example, hardly any theological or spiritual reflections extant on the role and vocation of marriage or family love. This does not necessarily mean that these things were unimportant to the Byzantines, merely that the old traditions of rhetorical reflection did not see them as centre-stage. The division of antique Greek society into public and private domains was also a factor that greatly inhibited any writing about domestic life. As women were traditionally regarded as occupying the 'private' domain, and rhetoric described the 'public' domain, the two trajectories do not often coincide. One has to approach issues of what marital life was like in early Byzantium, therefore, through other reflective lenses than the rhetorical tradition. One chief place in this regard would be the canonical texts that are concerned with marriage legislation and discipline. This, of course, is as unproductive for accessing the deeper questions, and perhaps as depressing, as it would be today to seek to define a spirituality of marriage purely by recourse to contemporary legal dossiers. The burgeoning amount of hagiographies, or 'Lives of the Saints', produced in later Byzantine literature gives ample proof that the categories of saintly existence had been well and truly commandeered by monastic ascetics and learned hierarchs who were defenders of the faith. Such hagiographies predominate to the extent that other types of figure have difficulty accessing the literary canon. But even then the traces remained, as we shall see when we consider some of the roles women saints play in the hagiographies later in this chapter.

STYLITES AND HERMITS: DWELLERS IN AN APOCALYPTIC LANDSCAPE

The typical Byzantine Saint's Life, however, celebrated the amazing exploits of monks who could demonstrate extraordinary feats of asceticism. Such literature was meant to be edifying and to advocate the monasteries attached to such saints as centres of spiritual counsel for others. Stylites, or ascetics who dwelt on top of pillars, were among the most famous 'athletes of God'. The fourth-century Syrian ascetic Symeon Stylites was the most well-known practitioner of this discipline of *stasis*, the practice of prayer over long hours in a motionless posture, but by the fifth century, there was even a stylite saint in the middle of the great capital at Constantinople. The Life of Daniel the Stylite was written by a contemporary and it focuses on his gifts of prophecy and the miracles of healing and intercession he is able to perform after his years of askesis. It is clear from most of the hagiographic narratives that the Byzantine saint usually occupied an important and sensitive position as a mediator between the common people, the patriarchal church authorities, and even the imperial court. Other ascetics at the capital immured themselves in small cells as a variant on the asceticism of *stasis*, and had food brought once a week by disciples. The role and character of the ascetic was drawn in such lurid colours partly because their lives were indeed 'extreme' in our sense of the word, and partly because the hagiographies are setting out as didactic literature to demonstrate the goal of *apatheia* which they expect the saints to manifest: that state of dispassion where a human being has transcended the weaknesses and limitations of the bodily condition. Celibacy was one of the first requirements of the road to dispassion, and so too fasting, and much prayer. We moderns may find the idea perplexing as a spiritual goal for Christianity, especially since the dominant theme of much reflection on the spiritual and moral life over this last hundred years has so firmly turned on the notions of compassionate social action. The Byzantine hagiographies represent another approach, different and certainly tangential but not necessarily opposite to that perspective, for although it may not be stated at the forefront of the hagiographies, the concepts of social mediation and philanthropy are central to the agenda here too. Even the most secluded ascetics were, in Byzantine thought, regarded as sustaining the security of the city and state by their constant prayers before God, and to this extent were often regarded as deserving imperial support and protection. What is at play in such 'extreme' narratives of asceticism is the depiction of the Christian life in apocalyptic terms. It is a different understanding of apocalyptic than may be apparent in the New Testament literature, but none the less still vital and active as a shaping force in this later period of Christian history. Athanasios of Alexandria, in his fourth-century treatise 'On the Incarnation of the Word', already points to the Christian celibates as those who have demonstrated the grace of the Spirit in an apocalyptic lifestyle. Those men and women who practise freely chosen celibacy are, he says, living against the flow of nature. They are already in an apocalyptic lifestyle such as envisaged by Jesus when he spoke of the saints and angels of God, in the Next Age, where they would 'neither marry nor be given in marriage' (Mark 12:25). This state of already living (in this age) in the conditions of the Next Age (the apocalyptic realisation of the Kingdom) was, for the Byzantine Church, abundantly demonstrated by virginity and monastic life. Other ascetic practices such as fasting, and immobility during prayer, and withdrawal from society, all underlined the same values – to invoke the conditions of the Next Age when the saints would no longer live in the body but solely by the grace of God. Even an aristocratic Byzantine court-poet, such as the fourteenth-century writer Manuel Philes, could pen a poem 'On Apatheia' as part of a long series of abstruse and dilettantish courtly poems commenting on the ancient desert literature. He writes:

> When you achieve the status of a completely
>   dispassionate person
> You have in all wisdom brought the buried soul to
>   resurrection,
> Which ever seeks to move to the light of the angels,
> Once it has shed the dust of passions and darkness.[1]

HAGIOGRAPHY AS BYZANTINE FOLK LITERATURE

Athanasios of Alexandria gave a massive momentum to the production of Byzantine hagiography by his creation of a best-seller in the mid fourth century: the *Life of Antony*. This narrative of the holy man Antony of Egypt depicted him as philosopher, ascetic, wonder-worker, and guardian of orthodoxy. It had the result of canonising Antony as 'the first monk', and was a text in the vanguard of the extraordinary explosion of ascetic non-urban Christianity along the Nile in the fourth century. His hagiography takes themes and devices from contemporary philosophical 'lives of the sophists' and merges the genre with abundant biblical motifs taken from the Old Testament accounts of the zealous prophets, as well as Gospel parallels. The iconography that soon began to parallel the increasing production of hagiographic texts abundantly demonstrates the important underlying principle of saintly 'bodilessness'. The icons of the ascetics depict them as surreally thin, almost spatially disembodied within this fleshly vehicle, a body that has become all but transparent to the light of the spirit. The saints are stretched against a background of golden mosaic, shimmering in an unearthly light ('sages standing in God's holy fire'). By virtue of their holy asceticism the saints are seen to have reached the state of dispassion (*apatheia*): at once the highest philosophical and moral goal, and a condition of being more with the angels than humans, and thus of being invested with powerful spiritual capacities as intercessors. As the saints' bodies become translucent and diminish, their spiritual powers as mediators of the grace of the next age to their contemporaries are seen as being increased. They are conceived, therefore, within the world-view of Byzantium, as the true aristocrats of the divine Emperor, albeit often in a lowly social condition. As most of the common people had little access to powerful patrons in late antiquity, it was a revolutionary idea within Byzantine hagiography that the local saints would demonstrate a God who had an ear open for the poor and dispossessed, and would answer their needs by supplying powerful, just, and accessible aristocratic patrons and defenders to hear them: that is the angels and local saints. So it was that the places of retirement of famous ascetics, their monasteries and later their tombs, became focal points of refuge and pilgrimage. For the Byzantine world-view, the saints were not merely considered in and of themselves as examples of divine grace purifying and abstracting the earthly condition, but particularly as examples of how God's power is at work in using selected men and women as channels of grace for the majority. The cult of the saints and their icons, from the fourth century onwards (and it is itself a continuance of the cult of martyrs from the primitive Christian period) grows with increasing momentum in the life and spirituality of the Byzantine Church.

TALES FROM THE DESERT

The catalogue of ascetics dominates the entire hagiographic genre. The stories from the deserts of Egypt and Syria show mainly men whose feats of endurance in fasting or prayer, demonstrate their transition to the status of 'Guide of the Next Age'. This story from the 'Sayings of the Desert Fathers' exactly illustrates the principle:

> One of the desert abbas came to see another abba. So this one said to his disciple: 'Cook us some lentils, and soak some of the bread in water for us.' And the disciple did this. But the two elders remained together discussing the things of the Spirit until noon of the following day. So once more the abba came to his disciple and said: 'Cook us some lentils, my son.' And the disciple replied: 'All has been held in readiness since yesterday.' And so it was the old men rose and ate their food.[2]

The two ascetic elders are so absorbed in the things of the Spirit that all earthly considerations, even the need for food, or the avoidance of the burning heat of the desert, falls away from them. Psychic gifts, such as clairvoyance, are regularly attributed to the saints. In the Life of the fifth-century Coptic saint, Abba Shenoute, we are given the following characteristic story illustrating how the elder knows what the disciples are thinking and mysteriously provides a meal for them in the capital city where he himself is a stranger. The story is so

obviously based on the Gospel account of Christ providing the
room of the Last Supper to the wonderment of the apostles
(Mark 14:12–16) that the Christ-saint parallelism is inescap-
able. For those who depend on the saint's spiritual powers, the
saint mediates the presence and power of the Lord:

> One day as Abba Shenoute was making his way to pray
> at the house of a friend of the emperor, the day was already
> growing late, and his monks had missed their mealtime.
> They were complaining among themselves: 'Our father
> will kill us if he continues at this pace. We must have a
> little drink of water . . .' Our father Abba Shenoute knew
> in the spirit what they were thinking and while he was
> walking along with them down a street in Constantinople,
> he touched a certain door which instantly opened. After he
> had entered he called in the monks of his party, saying:
> 'Enter and eat!' And when they came in too they found a
> dining room all prepared; the table laid out in exactly the
> same fashion as their monastery at home, with everything
> they needed laid out too, with bread, and two young monks
> with jugs ready to give them water . . . After they had left
> they said to him: 'Father, who were those two brothers
> who served us?' And Abba Shenoute said to them: 'Give
> glory to God who fed the prophet Daniel in the Lions' den,
> for today he has prepared his dining room for you; and
> those monks who served you were the angels of the Lord.'
> The disciples were filled with amazement, and glorified
> God and our father Shenoute.[3]

The stories in the desert tradition are miniature hagiographies dedicated to pedagogic moral purposes: to illustrate a
point of Scripture or a spiritual attitude to the readers. The
stories often turn around an encounter of a seeker and an
elder. The story of the Egyptian elder, Abba Joseph of Pane-
physis, serves as an example. It parallels the Gospel story of
the rich young man approaching Jesus (Mark 10:17–22):

> Abba Lot went to visit Abba Joseph and said to him: 'Abba,

I say my small office of prayers as best I can. I fast a little, I pray, and I meditate. As far as I can I live in peace, and I purify my thoughts as best I may. What else is there I can do?' Then the elder stood up and stretched out his hands towards heaven. His fingers became like ten lamps of fire, and he said to him in reply: 'If you will, you can become fire completely.'[4]

The hagiography of the ninth-century St Antony the Younger describes how the saint encounters another elder ascetic who has the power to disappear at will. Antony has to confirm the old man's presence in the room by tentatively reaching out to touch his robe with his foot. He spoke to him in amazement:

'Truly, master, men can see you when you wish it to be so, but according to your desire you are invisible to all.' And the old man gave him this moral as a response: 'What do you say? Are you yourself unable to do this thing? I tell you, if you have not yet attained to this state, you have not yet become a proper monk.'[5]

In the Life of the tenth-century saint Luke of Stiris the reader is told that St Luke habitually levitated two feet from the ground whenever he prayed,[6] and the hagiographic tradition associated with Shenoute describes him as flying to and fro between Alexandria and Constantinople on a shining cloud (like Elijah) to consult with the emperor or defend orthodoxy at the synods being held there.[7] Saints are traditionally expected to have powerful control over sickness and demons (not unrelated concepts in the mindset of antiquity) but also customarily show harmony with wild beasts, who come to assist them (lions help to dig the graves of the great ascetics and so on), in a theme that evokes the restoration of an Edenic condition in the wilderness inhabited by the saints of Christ. Such a theme of harmony with nature is continued throughout the eastern tradition, and can be seen exemplified in the life of one of the great Russian saints of early modern times, Seraphim of Sarov, who had tamed a wild bear that visitors used to see at play beside his forest hermitage in Russia. He is often depicted in his icons with the bear playing nearby. The saint heals the world not merely the soul.

HOLY WOMEN OF BYZANTIUM

Women saints who appear in Byzantine hagiographical narrative, chief among them Mary of Egypt, Macrina, Thais, or Syncletica, are typically described as having achieved 'manly' status by the rigour of their ascetical lives, and in their acquisition of dispassion are equally credited, along with the male saints, with psychic gifts and spiritual authority. Mary of Egypt is portrayed as a notorious prostitute who even travels with the pilgrims on the ship passage from Alexandria to Jerusalem. When she arrives in the holy city for the feast of Pascha, the hagiography tells us that she was prevented by invisible, angelic forces, from physically entering the church, and the shock of this propelled her into a conversion experience of such dramatic scope that she left and lived henceforth in the deserts of Judaea, unknown to anyone until the end of her life when God sent a priest to witness her final days and deliver the Eucharist to her. Mary is able with the sign of the cross to walk dry shod over the Jordan. This presentation of women as either virgins or repentant whores is part and parcel of the apocalyptic extremity of hagiographic genre. It does not command the whole picture, however, as several other types of female Byzantine figures emerge from a closer reading of the evidence and offer intriguingly different possibilities of iconic presentation. The genres of ascetical hagiography always remained dominant, but the stories canonising the holy Empresses of Byzantium such as Pulcheria and Eudoxia of the fifth century, or the ninth-century Theodora who defended the icons, all show that the genre was capable of elastic manipulation.

The royal hagiographies presented their female protagonists as 'defenders of orthodoxy' because of their efforts to defend the monks or preserve the independence of ecclesiastical councils.

Other aristocrats were lauded for their charitable works in building poor houses or endowing monasteries. The retirement of royalty into monastic life was a common enough experience in Byzantine history not to warrant particular mention, but it was always the liturgical custom to refer to the 'founder' of a religious house in every liturgy celebrated there, something like the western custom of a chantry chapel in a cathedral, and so the religious 'founder' in the Byzantine experience was a category that shared the honours equally between the monastic saint whose teaching formed the 'rule' of the house, and the aristocratic or imperial patron whose money allowed it to happen. In the hagiographies of the royal empresses these twin themes predominate, and in some cases such as the stories associated with Eudoxia, the protagonists are described as having revelatory dreams (the places of the discovery of relics are revealed to them) that explain their foundation of religious houses. In this way their role as wealthy benefactors of religion was harmonised with a personal charismatic role as 'vehicle of God', as if they exercised a royal prophetic office as it were, albeit at one remove. The Byzantine world regarded some element of clairvoyance (at least the ability to receive divine intimations in dreams) as a standard expectation for the saints, who had the function in life of interpreting the divine will for others as spiritual guides. To this day, in Orthodox tradition, the saintly elder (the Starets or Starissa) will be regarded as primarily a confessor and guide for numerous pilgrims who will come to seek him or her out from wherever they have retreated, and the task of hearing the burdens of their hearts and comforting the sorrows of their lives becomes a final stage in what is regarded as the many forms of askesis necessary to achieve the perfect image of Christ.

From the fifth to the ninth centuries a genre of Byzantine hagiography presented the Lives of holy women who entered male monasteries, disguised as men, and excelled in every ascetical task. Always, at the time of the washing of the body in death, the subterfuge is discovered, and the monastery is in wonderment at how a woman was able to sustain such a rigorous life of asceticism. These stories, which have recently (not particularly accurately) been called 'transvestite hagiographies', have been the focus of modern interest in so far as they reveal social conditions for women in the Middle Byzantine era. Their predominant concern as hagiographies is to demonstrate the patriarchal principle that such women ascetics are endowed with a 'manly soul', but if they do reveal anything particular to women's spirituality, it is perhaps that the saint customarily remains unmoved by the opinions of others in the community. The scorn and disregard of these 'lowly monks' (often presumed to be weak eunuchs by the rest of the community) does not deflect them from the single-minded search for purity of soul under the eye of God. In the desert tradition a few of the great teachers were ammas (desert mothers), rather than abbas. Sarah and Syncletica are important among them, and their collected sayings demonstrate that perhaps they even had an assembly of disciples (presumably female too) gathered around them in their lifetimes, since such female hagiographic paradigms as the Life of Mary of Egypt have no real 'sayings tradition' associated with their chief characters at all, and serve merely to demonstrate archetypal principles and attitudes. The accumulation of a sayings tradition from a female desert teacher is far more significant in showing that early Christianity had not entirely forgotten the importance of women's religious experience in a predominantly patriarchal environment.

DOMESTIC SAINTS IN BYZANTIUM

The similar idea of heroic fidelity to one's principles, even in the face of overwhelming oppressive force, is also noticed in the women saints' Lives from the ninth and tenth centuries that are more 'domestic' in character than the earlier monastic hagiographies. The theme of the abusive husband whose tyranny is a real martyrdom as far as the wife is concerned, is present in some of the Lives of female saints from this era, giving a window onto medieval society that is not often opened in other sources. It could even be the case that the compilers of such hagiographies of abused wives deliberately set out to reform the abuses of domestic violence that were otherwise passing unnoticed in the life of the Church. Matrona of Perge escaped her desperately unhappy marriage in the fifth century to become a famous abbess of a community in Constantinople. It was here that her cult of sanctity was preserved at least until the twelfth century. The Life of Theoktiste of Lesbos describes a woman who had entered a convent as a young woman and was shortly afterwards abducted in a raid on her town by Cretan pirates (a common plague on life in the Aegean islands). She preferred to escape while the slave ship was taking on water at Paros (then supposedly uninhabited) and lived the life of a solitary island recluse for the next thirty-five years, until one day she told her story to a hunter who was wandering in the wilderness of the inner island. The hagiography adopts elements from the more famous tale of Mary of Egypt, but also demonstrates enough independent details to suggest that here was indeed a new hagiographic tale that gave encouragement to a population who lived in fear of Islamic slave raiders, and valued the story of a woman of uncommon valour who lived out her monastic vocation in time of war and at such personal cost.

Finally, the Lives of two other tenth-century saints, Mary the Younger and Thomais of Lesbos, are rare forms of hagiography celebrating the sanctity of married women. Both of them are also victims of abusive relations. The hagiography insists that marriage and childbearing do not exclude them from the ranks of the saints, but the monastic paradigm of hagiography is already by this period so strong that both these candidates for saintly honours endure rather than celebrate their marital condition. The wealthy Mary the Younger is praised for achieving sanctity by her philanthropy to the poor and by her humane attitude to her household servants, but it is this very charitableness and good-heartedness that so rouses the anger of her 'empty-headed' husband against her that he finally beats her to death. The lower-class Thomais is similarly beaten to death, as the last stage in a miserable and oppressive existence sharing the house of an ill-tempered bully; but the narrative in her case claims an exceptional thing – that her murder was in fact a real martyrdom, and she deserves the respect afforded to ancient apostolic saints because of her persever-ance in a ministry of compassionate prayer, refusing to be deflected from the dignity of a Christian soul by her brutalising treatment. That such a claim was being made in the tenth century by these kind of married women's Lives is perhaps an indication that the Church was deliberately forming a novel kind of literary genre in hagiography to correct some of the abuses of domestic violence it knew to be common in society. It is noteworthy that neither of the women saints achieved large-scale fame in the subsequent hagiographic tradition, even though both Lives end with a recounting of miracles of cures taking place at the site of their tombs in the capital city. The celebration of domestic heroism might well have had a very important role to play in modelling new attitudes to marital relations and familial responsibility, but it did not make the new hagiographies much of a match for the old and ever-popular genres that could call upon an array of extreme stories to demonstrate an 'otherworldliness' that these later domestic narratives could not.

Mary the Younger, far from being a celibate ascetic, was a rich and kindly benefactor of the poor who suffered great vio-lence. Her life was a small-scale tragedy, an issue of bravery and consistency in the face of oppression. As the hagiographer argued:

> If perfume is poured out, even in a secret place, it cannot go unnoticed for the very fragrance will betray it: and so it is with a person actively living the virtuous life. The works themselves will proclaim it openly. Just so, this most revered woman Mary, who served the Lord in a fervent spirit, could not pass unnoticed.[8]

The old-style hagiographies, with monks and martyrs bat-tling demons for the survival of the Church and the healing of local people, retained their appeal throughout the Byzantine centuries, a testimony, no doubt, to the fact that the common people wanted to hear about sanctity achieved in starkly simple and apocalyptic terms. This is what the hair-raising stories of endurance are meant to illustrate. It was an appealing way of graphically illustrating the character of Christian sanctity, but one that also ran the risk of abstracting the 'saint' from the realities and complexities of human culture. It was a cliché that later hagiographic texts, woodenly plagiarising the earlier ones, fell into more and more.

It was largely because the standard Byzantine hagiographies always appealed to a similar set of *topoi*, or narrative archetypes, that without question the lives of monastic heroes of asceticism prevailed in their pages. Yet there were sufficient indications always present that other things apart from ascetic endurance were important: the ability to be compassionate, and offer hospitality, and the ability to serve as a guide and comforter for one's fellow seekers, not least among them. The witness of the few tales of married women saints that survive from Byzantium leave one with a sense of sadness in the face of such oppression, a domestic terrorism that still endures as one of the pervasive hidden forms of violence against women in urban societies all over the world, whether developed or undeveloped. The existence of these few exemplars of domestic hagiography, however, signal that the genre was capable of trying to address social abuses it saw in its contemporary society. It does not so much present the victims as passive models for emulation, but rather wishes to explode the abuse by 'naming and shaming'. The protagonists of these few hagiographies are glorified not as classical martyrs, but as women of courage who refused to be deflected from the call to compassion, even though no one was willing, in return, to come to their assistance. Theirs was a resolution that could not be beaten into submission by the violent and small-minded. It was such hidden springs that gave to these lives their extraordinary significance for the Byzantines, that rendered the base coinage of ordinary existence into the gold standard of

faithful discipleship in whatever condition they found themselves. Such things remain perennially instructive in a world
where a conniving silence is often the temptation (the desire
for the quiet life) of those who are otherwise good and merciful,
but whose failure to speak out can often allow evil and injustice
to flourish. The Byzantine hagiographies, very much drawn in
lurid colours and cartoonlike in plot, can often amuse as much
as they disturb us. Sometimes, however, they have the force
to catch us unaware and offer us moving instruction in the
levels of courage that have sometimes been required of faithful
disciples.

7. THE LUMINOUS SILENCE OF HESYCHASM

THE LIGHT EMITTED BY THE SOUL

Evagrios and Gregory Nazianzen had spoken of a spiritual state where the purified soul could even see its own radiance as it prayed. The Byzantine spiritual writers of the late tenth century and afterwards were taken up by the concept and experience of such a mystical transfiguration in light, so much so that the idea of luminous metamorphosis came to be a distinctive mark of a new spiritual 'school', that of Byzantine Hesychasm. It takes its name from the traditional term for stillness (*hesychia*) which by now had also become a common word for 'monk'. The 'Hesychast' movement is, therefore, more a restatement of traditional monastic spirituality than a wholly new kind of Greek Christian spirituality, but even so it has distinctive new emphases all of its own. In its origins, especially with Symeon the New Theologian whom we shall shortly consider, it is a monastic protest against the formalism of other sections of the Church and the imperial court, and this can explain some of the marked differences between the later Greek and Latin church traditions for, unlike the West which was at this period beginning its long period of scholasticisation, the Hesychast movement prioritised monastic experience over philosophical speculation in regard to the faith. Given that the East never suffered from the crisis of Reformation which progressively weakened the religious orders of the West but instead entered a long period of subjection to Islam, in which the monasteries acted as important oases of Christian teaching and culture, the rise of Hesychasm meant that Byzantine theology came to its archetypal 'statement' during this period, and was definitively marked by monastic Hesychast ideas. In terms of the concept of what theology was, Hesychasm ensured that it would ever after in the Byzantine tradition be seen as an extension of the spiritual life of the individual and community, never as divorced from it, as an intellectual game, or a missionary strategy.

The concept of spiritual 'stillness' can be seen already in Evagrios, and is rooted in ancient anthropological doctrines that regard the essential human person as composite, fragile, and always tending to diffraction and dissolution. The *hegemonikon*, or dominant aspect of the human composite, is *nous*: the spiritual aspect of the psychological life. The presidency of the *nous*, however, is subject to disruption by *epithymia* – powerful urges both bodily and emotive. The direction of the inner life is a fraught thing because, in monastic belief, the demons also war within the bodily and psychic life, trying to counteract the asceticism of the monk, and disrupt the spiritual influences of Christ's grace.

Stillness of soul is achieved by fasting, prayer, and retiring recollection. These things quieten outward desires, in the pursuit of silencing the clamour of the mind and the soul: the overall aim is to achieve the stillness where the voice of God can be heard. So far this is a sober restatement of much that could be found in Evagrios or the other desert teachers, but in later Byzantine Hesychast thought the predominant emphasis moved from ascetical 'governance' to a more pronounced theory of spiritual 'vision'. This turn into a more developed mysticism of vision is seen first in Symeon the New Theologian (d. 1022), and comes to a peak in the Hesychastic dispute proper, particularly represented in the thirteenth century by Gregory Palamas in his controversy with the Italo-Byzantine monk Barlaam of Calabria. The figure of Gregory of Sinai completes the ranks of the three most important of the 'Hesychast' teachers, although Symeon, strictly speaking, lived before the movement and is more accurately designated one of its important progenitors.

SYMEON THE NEW THEOLOGIAN (949–1022)

Symeon was born in 949 to an aristocratic Byzantine family.[1] As an old man he laments that his family never gave him 'the affection commonly expected of kin'. It is possible that as a child he was made a eunuch for future service in the imperial palace at Constantinople. In 960 he was sent to the capital for his education. A few years afterwards Symeon's uncle and protector, a high-ranking politician in the city, was assassinated in the revolution of 963, but the young man's career still developed and soon he was admitted to senatorial rank, in daily attendance at the palace. It was in his twenties that he first encountered the monk Symeon Eulabes who, though not ordained, acted as a father-confessor to a group of young aristocrats in the city. He was an odd but generously charismatic figure. Symeon describes his own lifestyle as decadently worldly but he visited the old monk regularly and followed the short rule of morning and night prayers that he gave him along with reading the occasional spiritual book. In 969 he records in his writings an event which he (later) came to regard as decisive in his conversion. One evening as he was praying he had a vision of two radiant lights, one absorbed in the overwhelming brightness of the other.[2] He interpreted the event as a spiritual vision of how his spiritual father was interceding for him before Christ at the very moment he was making his own prayers. Seven years later, another palace coup in 976 initiated a sequence of events that changed his life permanently. The young prince Basil II was set on the throne under the regent Basil. Symeon's family seem to have been marked out by the new power-élite as a hostile element. His own political career was terminated and he took refuge with his spiritual father at the Studite monastery. Here he tells us that once again he experienced an overwhelming vision of light. He saw the radiance of Christ, directly, and this became for him a definitive conversion point. It marked his permanent entrance into the monastic state. His political connections made it possible for him soon afterwards to move to the St Mamas monastery at Constantinople, near to his spiritual father, where three years later, in 979–80, he was appointed the *higumen*, or abbot. Being still a powerful and wealthy patron, Symeon substantially refurbished St Mamas, and at this time began to deliver the traditional morning spiritual teachings (catecheses) to his monks of the community. These have survived as the central body of his work. Much of his teaching is traditional Studite monastic philosophy,[3] but he has a definite emphasis on the necessity for direct personal experience in the life of the Spirit. He demanded that immense reliance should be placed on a spiritual father, and argued that without affective experience, a person's prayer was suspect. This strong stress on direct experience of the Spirit seems to have caused no little conflict among his subordinates, some of whom were possibly lax in their spiritual lives, though others held genuine suspicions against someone they came to regard as an inexperienced and unbalanced charismatic zealot. Between 995 and 998 a large number of his community broke out in revolt against Symeon's discipline and teachings. A legal attempt to have him dismissed from his position failed. But a few years later the Emperor himself seems to have instigated moves against him. In 995 Symeon was censured for 'excessive veneration' of his now dead father-confessor, and in 1003 an attempt was made to disgrace Symeon as an incompetent theologian. He gave as good as he got, and in turn lambasted the court-bishops as desiccated formalists who had no experience of the mysteries of the theology they were claiming to adjudicate.[4] He made his position clear at this time: without having experienced the highest levels of prayer, in impassibility, and having witnessed a vision of the divine light, no one should ever dare to teach or speak for the Christian tradition. His challenge was recognised by the synod of bishops, and the long-running hostility culminated in 1005 with a sentence of deposition, an order for his house arrest, and his subsequent banishment from the city. He continued to write in a small oratory near Constantinople, attended by a select band of his loyal disciples. It was here that he composed a collection of

'Hymns of Divine Love', containing some of the most rhapsodic and mystical poetry in all Byzantine tradition. *The Hymns*, along with the *Catecheses*, are his greatest works. He died, aged seventy-three, in 1022, and so great was the controversy surrounding his name that it was thirty years before his disciples managed to bring his remains back for burial at the capital. In later centuries his works became treasured as authoritative writings on prayer on Mount Athos, and it was there that Gregory Palamas and Gregory of Sinai encountered them. In his robust demands for an experiential theology in the face of increasingly deadening bureaucratic formalisms they recognised a man after their own hearts. In his enthusiastic insistence on personal spiritual experience and his advocacy of the idea of divine grace as a transfiguring light – not merely an analogy, but a real experience of God for the person who advanced in prayer, comparable to the luminous transfiguration the disciples witnessed on Thabor – Symeon struck chords in his later admirers that would flourish into a coherent spiritual doctrine. In Symeon's hands, however, it is more the case that we are dealing with a profoundly passionate mystic and apologist. The *Hymns of Divine Love* address the Christ directly, person to person in a manner that is highly unusual for literature of this period, but which was to seize the imagination of the Church, and become, afterwards, a standard image of highly personal dialogue with the Saviour:

A Hymn of Divine Eros

Master how could I describe the vision of your face?
How could I ever speak of the ineffable contemplation of
  your beauty?
How could mere words contain
One whom the World could never contain?
How could anyone ever express your love for humankind?
I was sitting in the light of a lamp that was shining down
  on me,
lighting up the darkness and shadows of the night,
where I was sitting to all appearances busy in reading,

> but more engaged in meditating on the ideas and
>   concepts.
> While I was meditating on such things, master,
> suddenly you yourself appeared from on high,
> far greater than the Sun itself,
> shining brilliantly from the heavens down into my
>   heart . . .
> What intoxication of the Light! What swirlings of fire!
> What dancing of the flame of you and your glory within
>   me,
> wretched man that I am.[5]

His last line shows how consciously Symeon is modelling the
account of his luminous vision on the version of the theophany
in the Temple in Isaiah 6, where the presence of God fills the
prophet with a deep sense of his own unworthiness. It is
the same with Symeon, the sense of unworthiness is overwhelmed by a deeper sense of divine commissioning, and the
realisation that God meets with humans for the cause of their
liberation and salvation:

> O my Creator and maker, shelter me under your hand,
> Do not abandon me, or be angry towards me.
> Do not take account of my great laxity,
> But make me worthy, through your light, even to the
>   end,
> That I may walk boldly in the path of your
>   commandments . . .
> For your compassion is great, and your mercy ineffable.
> Take me, even as I am, in the shelter of your hand my
>   Saviour.[6]

For Symeon, the mystical vision of God is not reserved for
the élite and the holy, but is rather a grace which God gives
unmerited to those who can repent with a genuine passion.
The mystic, in his understanding, is thus the ordinary
Christian who has supreme confidence to stand in God's presence, trusting entirely in penitence, not in good deeds. The

mystic is not a stage of 'perfection' distinct from the ordinary
run of Christian life, but a full realisation of the grace of God
given to the 'broken of heart'. The mystic, in this sense, is at
the heart of the gospel experience, not on its periphery. It is
one of the most important insights of the Byzantine spiritual
tradition as a whole.

Symeon is conscious of his own failings, yet it is these very
things which give wing to his confidence, for it is his need
which calls forth the abundant mercy of God:

> Of sinners I am the chief, O my Christ [1 Tim. 1:15] and
> When I found myself at the bottom of the abyss
> I cried out for your mercy, for I realized the extent of my
>   evil . . .
> I wept, I shed rivers of tears from my eyes, and cried out
>   with inexpressible groans
> And from your ineffable heights you heard me
> Where I lay in the depths of the abyss . . .
> And leaving all the Powers that surround you
> You passed in haste through all the visible Cosmos
> To stoop down to the place where I was lying,
> Straightway bringing me your light, casting out the
>   darkness
> And reviving me with your divine breath . . .
> You captivated me with your beauty and your love.
> How you wounded me, transforming me utterly.[7]

The one thing that called forth Symeon's chief denunciations
was the tendency of spiritual sloth that masqueraded as
common sense. It was the attitude he found all around him in
the bourgeois Church of the Byzantine middle ages. He rails
against theologians or Christians who think that a relationship with God is only for the saints, and usually for saints of
a different, previous age; that this generation cannot expect
to have the charismatic gifts of God readily accessible to it,
and ought to rest content in a faithfulness to the memories of
the great acts of God in the past. For Symeon, this is the
quintessential blasphemy, the avoidance of the invitation to

encounter with God which is the essential dynamic of the
spiritual life:

> Let us all earnestly seek the only one who is capable
> of freeing us from our bonds.
> Let us long for him with all our hearts,
> for his beauty fills all thoughts and hearts with wonder,
> it wounds our souls and gives them wings to fly to God,
>   to be united fast with him forever.
> So, my brothers, run by your deeds towards him . . .
> Do not contradict what we are telling you, deceiving
>   yourselves.
> Do not claim that it is impossible these days
>   to receive the Spirit of God.
> Do not pretend that you can find salvation without this
>   experience.
> Do not claim that a Christian can possess the Spirit
>   without necessarily being aware of it.
> Do not claim that God is not able to be seen by men.
> Do not claim that men cannot lay eyes on the divine
>   light.
> Do not claim that this is not possible in this day and age.
> It is never impossible my friends.
> On the contrary it is a thing most possible for those who
>   desire it.
> But you must lead a life purified of passions,
> and have eyes that themselves are purified.[8]

Symeon's ability to pass so easily in his lyrical way between
the sense of God's absolute transcendence, and the immanent
closeness of the divine presence is nowhere seen more dramati-
cally than in his *Eucharistic Hymns*. Symeon saw the reception
of the Eucharist as a quintessential example of his doctrine of
the direct experience of God's sensible presence. He instructed
his disciples never to contemplate receiving the Eucharist if
their hearts had not first been moved to tears, so strong was
his insistence that formalism in religion is fatal to the spiritual
life. The reception of the Eucharist he describes as a holistic

absorption into the presence of Christ and, in that very action, a primary form of the divinisation of the creature by reception of the Godhead's own presence:

> My blood has been mingled with your blood,
> And I come to the understanding
> of how I have also been made one with your own godhead.
> I have become your own most pure body:
> A member of that body, scintillating and truly sanctified,
> radiant, transparent, and light-emitting . . .
> What was I once? And what have I now become?
> How awesome to think of it.
> Where shall I sit? What shall I touch?
> Where shall I rest these limbs that have become your
>   very own?
> These members that are now so terrible and so mighty,
> how shall I use them, to what work shall I now set them?[9]

Symeon's highly personal and passionate mystical sense of God's presence, and his robust apologetic against clerical religious formalism made him many enemies in his time, but won him the abiding admiration of generations of Greek monks that followed, especially on Mount Athos, where his radiant teachings on mystical prayer, and his insistence on the importance of a spiritual father-guide for the serious seeker, became constitutive parts of later Athonite monasticism, and prepared the way for the development of Hesychasm proper.

ST GREGORY OF SINAI (*c.* 1255–1346)

Gregory Koukoulos, now generally known as Gregory of Sinai, was born some time between 1255 and 1265 on what is now the Turquoise coast, and what was then the still heavily Greek shores of Asia Minor. He belonged to a wealthy family but was captured and enslaved in a Turkish pirate raid on his town. After eventually being ransomed, Gregory left his family and set off for Cyprus where he became a novice monk, and then moved on to Sinai where he committed himself to the full monastic profession. He found the Sinai traditions of prayer too conflicted for his comfort, and left the arguments in his monastery to go on further researches into the state of the spiritual life in other major centres of the eastern Christian world. Travelling to Crete he studied the nature of interior prayer with a spiritual master there known as Arsenios. It was here that he was advised to make the Jesus Prayer the centre of all his spiritual endeavours. The constant and slow repetition of the phrase: 'Lord Jesus Christ, Son of God, have mercy on me', was given to him to serve as the very pulse of his spiritual consciousness. This use of the Jesus Prayer was, of course, an ancient tradition from the time of the early desert fathers, but Gregory describes his admission into the tradition almost as if it were the rediscovery of a lost mystery. The general state of spirituality in the Church of his day seems to have become highly dependent on set vocal prayers. His disciple and biographer, the patriarch Kallistos, says that when Gregory came to Mount Athos, even there the spiritual tradition had been entirely subsumed by devotional services and acts of asceticism.

Appropriating the tradition he had relearned from the ancient master Makarios, Gregory strongly advocated the use of the Jesus Prayer, and related it explicitly to the heart's inner sensibility and even to the very physical beat of the heart, considering it as if it were a metronome keeping time in parallel with the breath's own vocalisation of the words of the Jesus Prayer. He thus became one of the great Hesychast proponents of the 'Prayer of the Heart' as it concretely shaped and defined the Hesychast movement. It is this tradition of the Prayer of the Heart, at last rendered synonymous with the Jesus Prayer, that has passed on to the Orthodox Church in the modern age as its most central tradition of spiritual consciousness.

Gregory moved on to the monastic colonies of Mount Athos, where he chose to live in a small hermitage, the skete of Magoula, near the larger Philotheou monastery. This was a time when Gregory Palamas was also a monk on Mount Athos, but it is unknown whether the two ever met. Gregory (of Sinai) refused to take part in the theological controversies that engendered 'Hesychast theology' either in Sinai or on Athos, although it is clear from his writings that he shared more or less the same ideas as Palamas. Troublesome military raids on Athos, which were becoming more frequent as the Turks moved in to settle the Asia Minor coast in the declining years of the Byzantine Empire, caused him to leave the Halkidiki peninsula in 1325. He eventually settled in Paroria in Thrace around 1330 and built a monastery of his own design in the relative safety of Mount Katakekryomene, the wild regions on the border between the Byzantine Empire and Bulgaria. As a young monk he had a reputation for fierce asceticism, now as he had grown old with other hermits clustering around him seeking advanced spiritual guidance, he was chiefly known for his deep joy and kindness, characteristics which are marked in his writing. In this last stage of his life, with the patronage of the Bulgarian Tsar, John Alexander, he was able to edit and publish his collected works. The large group of monastic disciples which had gathered around him, both Greek-speaking and Slav, passed on his spiritual tradition in both language families of the Byzantine world, ensuring its important influence for centuries to come throughout Orthodoxy, a factor which was confirmed when five of his treatises were included in the *Philokalia*,[10] the eighteenth-century Orthodox Church's compilation of authoritative monastic writings on prayer. The traditional date of Gregory's death is 27 November 1346.

Gregory adopted the somewhat surprising teaching that the best posture for hesychast prayer was one where the practitioner sat down on a low stool, about nine inches high. This was more novel to Byzantine ears than might appear today, for it had been the ancient and unbroken eastern practice to make one's prayer in a standing position with the hands upraised. The shoulders were to be bowed, and the back bent over with the head more or less tucked into the chest. This followed the spiritual tradition of an earlier teacher,

Nicephoros of Mount Athos, who in the late thirteenth century
had written a little manual *On Vigilance and the Guarding of
the Heart.*[11] The oddly constricting posture, so unlike the Zen
postures, for example, was probably connected with something
that Gregory of Sinai develops in his turn – the close corre-
lation of the breathing with the vocalisation of the words of
the Jesus Prayer. It is, of course, nigh on impossible to
synchronise the breathing in and out with a loud public vocalisation of the prayer, but Gregory is here envisaging the
personal dimension of a sibilant and almost silent vocalisation
of the words: 'Lord Jesus Christ Son of God have mercy on me
(a sinner)'. And at times when the attention is straying, he
advises the more distinct vocalisation of the words[12] – as long
as it is done slowly and calmly.

His predecessor Nicephoros had offered his advice on
posture, intending to constrict the breathing, especially at the
start of prayer, so as to force the attentiveness of the body, to
capture it, as it were, and bring the mind down as a captive
into the domain of the heart. In a graphic way this capturing
of the restless mind by the closely attentive psychic consciousness, was physically brought about by the pulling of the mind
down into the inner person, through constricting and then
focusing the breathing. One presumes, though the writers do
not specifically mention it, that the tight posture would be
relaxed once attention had been gained in the course of prayer.
Otherwise it is difficult to see how the position could be sustained physically for very long, and Gregory even suggests
that the method is not being performed properly if it is not
hurting. For Gregory, the taming of the breathing is more a
manner of slowing down the rhythm of breaths, closing the
mouth a little, and synchronising the breath with the evocation
of the Holy Name of Jesus. The purpose of it all is psychic
concentration, the stilling of the teeming thoughts, and then
the opening up from this into a greater dimension of reality.
Gregory describes this as coming, usually, with a feeling of
warmth in the heart. The Name, as was the case with the
ancient biblical understanding of the sacred name of the Lord

God of Israel (a name that could never be pronounced aloud except by the High Priest in the inner sanctum on the Day of Atonement), was far more than a mere mantra or title; it was itself an evocation of the divine presence. Gregory wishes the monk to draw in the spiritual invocation of the divine Jesus with every breath, not merely to focus the spiritual attention of the one who prays the Jesus Prayer, but more to consecrate the synthetic union of the single spiritual and physical dimension that constitutes a person. This unitive force of the presence consecrating the disciple at prayer, is called by the Hesychasts the movement of 'deification'. It is a sacramental, incarnational mystery of how the divine Lord lifts the one who prays into the transforming presence of his own holiness, just as the Logos once took flesh in time and space, and continues to take flesh across time and space in the mysteries of the Eucharist. The hesychast at prayer, therefore, is like the process of a eucharistic transfiguration into the mystery of Jesus. Gregory describes prayer as 'sacrifice on the noetic altar'[13] and as an interior liturgy celebrated in the holy place of the heart; a sanctuary which Christ himself illuminates brilliantly:

> The Kingdom of God is like the tabernacle that was built by God and whose pattern he revealed to Moses (Exod. 25:40). It too has an inner and outer sanctum. All who are priests of grace can enter into the first court, but the second, the noetic sanctum, is reserved for those who in this life have already attained the divine darkness of theological wisdom, and have celebrated the trinitarian liturgy passing into that tabernacle that Jesus himself has built,[14] and where he acts as their consecrator and High Priest before the Trinity, illuminating them more and more profoundly with the light of his own brilliance.[15]

Gregory uses the dynamic (and highly Christological) image of describing the disciples at prayer as being like pregnant mothers: 'Whoever has received grace is like a woman impregnated, conceiving child by the Holy Spirit.'[16] This assimilation to Christ is not merely a spiritual transfiguration, it draws in the whole incarnate reality of a person. Prayer is that process of the deification of creatures by the transfiguring presence of God: 'When you have been renewed in the Spirit and kept the gift of grace, you will be transfigured and embodied in Christ; and you will then experience that state of deification that transcends nature and all our attempts to describe it.'[17] Gregory clearly envisages an ongoing process in the life of prayer so that the person who advances knows more and more of the inner mysteries of the Spirit, and comes to a state where words are less and less operative, and so his preferred symbol is the soul's 'rapture to light':

> What I mean by rapture is the complete ascent of the soul's force towards the majesty of the glory of God, now revealed as a seamless unity. Or you could describe it as a pure and all encompassing ascent towards that infinite power that dwells in light. It is not merely the heavenly rapture of the soul's powers, it also comprises the complete transcendence of the sensible world itself. This deep desire for God ... is a spiritual intoxication that arouses all our longing ... It is truly an intoxication of the spirit driving on our natural thoughts towards higher realities, and detaching the senses from their attention to visible realities.[18]

The condition of prayer that begins with the warming of the heart, changes into something else with the advent of God's higher gifts:

> When we are beginners, prayer is like a fire of joy kindled in the heart. For the perfect it is like a strong and sweetly perfumed radiance.[19]

It is in this higher state of illumination that the transcendence of material images, both in words and mental states, is accomplished:

> According to our theologians, noetic prayer, that is the

pure prayer of the angels, is essentially the great wisdom inspired in us by the Holy Spirit. The sign that we have attained such prayer is when our intellective vision is completely liberated from all paradigmatic forms, and when the intellect sees neither itself nor any other thing in material fashion. On the contrary, it is often drawn away even from its own senses by the light that is at work within it. It grows immaterial and is filled with spiritual luminosity. By an ineffable joining together, it becomes a single spirit with God. (1 Cor. 6:17).[20]

In many aspects of his doctrine, Gregory is clearly following the tradition of the Syrian master Makarios. Images such as the impregnation by the Spirit of God, the intoxication of divine love, and the fire within the heart, are explicitly taken from that tradition. But his importance lies not so much in his innovation (or lack of it), but his powers of synthesis. For to the ancient tradition of the Prayer of the Heart, he adds a very strong stress on the simple practicalities of the Jesus Prayer as that anchor and rope that stabilises the soul even as it ascends in ecstasy before the face of God in the heavenly tabernacle. After Gregory, the Jesus Prayer was no longer seen as a basic stage for beginners, but the quintessence of advanced prayer. Not only did the repetition of the words calm and still the soul and warm the heart, but the theological meaning of that prayer encapsulated the entire gospel experience: that Christ, our God, was first and foremost the Saviour of sinners, and chose to enter and eat with those who were conscious of their failures, as their doctor and liberator. As was the case with the tax collector in the Temple, by this heartfelt prayer of love and repentance, a disciple could emerge: 'made one again with God that day' (cf. Luke 18:9–14).

ST GREGORY PALAMAS (*c.* 1296–1359)

Gregory Palamas is the most famous and most specifically 'theological' of the founders of Hesychasm. He was born in

Constantinople *circa* 1296. His family were aristocrats closely involved with the imperial court, and the young child seemed destined for imperial service himself, but he decided to pursue a monastic vocation and so strongly advocated it in his family that his two brothers came with him, and later his sisters and his mother also adopted monastic profession. Some time around 1316 Gregory and his brothers left the city to join the Athonite monks. He stayed for a short time at Vatopedi monastery and then at the Great Lavra. He finally joined the small community of monks who lived in the skete of Glossia, a tiny dependent community on Athos that gave him a supportive family context and provided a focused concentration on advanced techniques of prayer. Here he was taught hesychastic techniques. Turkish pirate raids against Athos caused him to retire to the nearby city of Thessalonike, where he was ordained a priest in 1326. He spent some time after that in seclusion as a mountain hermit before finally returning to Athos in 1331. In 1336 Palamas heard of the writings of an Italo-Byzantine monk called Barlaam of Calabria. Barlaam's theology, abstracted from his readings of the sixth-century writer Dionysios the Areopagite, laid immense stress on the absolute 'unknowability' of God, and advocated a scholastic systematic method to elucidate what it was that theology could legitimately affirm. He saw the developments that were taking place in the western Church under the stimulus of philosophic reasoning, and was part of a larger movement in the Byzantine world that thought progressive reforms might be made on the basis of this approach. To Barlaam, the stiffest opposition to his vision of a Greek world renewed by western scholastic methodology, was Mount Athos. The monks of Athos had already become something like the general conscience of the Byzantine Church, but as far as Barlaam was concerned they were ignorant recidivists. His doctrine of the absolute unknowability of God had been challenged by these simple monks who claimed to see the divine light in their prayers, and experience the presence of the transcendent God as a friend speaking to a friend. What is more, the same monks set the insights gained in mystical prayer on a far higher plane than any insight about God gained by logic or reason. Barlaam made a counter-attack on their mysticism as world-withdrawal, and caricatured the Hesychast insistence that all theology is subservient to prayer. He lampooned the secret doctrine of the Hesychast school, especially Gregory of Sinai's teachings on the focus of the eyes on the inner place of the heart, the control of breathing, and the claim to see the divine light. He dismissed the Hesychasts as 'Navel-Psychics' (*Omphalopsychoi*). For Barlaam the divine reality was entirely transcendent, and any claim to have comprehended the Godhead in any way, or worse to have 'seen the divine light' was a blasphemous reduction of the divinity to earthly images. Gregory Palamas took up the challenge to defend the honour, and the credibility, of the Athonite spiritual tradition. In the course of his local defence, he soon realised that matters fundamental to the entire Christian tradition were at stake: issues that had been in conflict even in the earliest centuries of the Church: how could Christianity affirm the absolute transcendence of its God, while simultaneously maintaining the intimate connection of the deity with the creation? The master-idea that organises all Gregory's theological and spiritual writing is a vigorous defence of the principle of the incarnate activity of God: that in Jesus the divinity is so intimately joined to the human race that it is given to Christian mystics to have a transcendent union with God which is always mediated through the earthly perceptions of the creature, analogous to the manner in which the full deity of the Logos was mediated fully through the authentic humanity of Jesus. The favourite of all the Hesychast images to express the manner in which humanity (that of Jesus, and that of the disciple in prayer) can serve as a bounded, but unlimited medium of divine grace, was the figure of Jesus himself, bodily transfigured in the divine light of Thabor.

Gregory had several great supporters in his controversial battles. The heads of the powerful Athonite monasteries encouraged him to write on their behalf, and he enjoyed the support of numerous Byzantine bishops, including the three

patriarchs of Constantinople active in his time: Isidore I, Kallistos I (a former disciple of Gregory of Sinai), and Philotheos
Kokkinos (who wrote a hagiographic praise of Palamas after
his death). Palamas also had strong secular support in the
person of his patron General John Katakouzenos, the head of
one of the most powerful aristocratic families in Constantinople who was soon to assume the throne at the capital. The
argument between Barlaam and Gregory captured the imagination of a very wide and public audience. Gregory composed
his first major writing in 1338 entitled *Triads in Defence of
the Holy Hesychasts*.[21] At a synod held among the clerics on
Athos in 1340–1, his work was approved, and the monks also
issued their own supportive statement (probably drafted by
Palamas) called the 'Hagioritic Tome'. In this document the
light of Thabor is connected, eschatologically, with the light of
the Kingdom to come, and those who witness it here on earth
are portrayed as those who in the present age witness the
charism of the prophets of the Lord. Patriarchal councils in
Constantinople added their agreement in 1341, 1347, and
1351, all endorsing Palamas as an authoritative spokesman
for the Orthodox tradition. It did not all go his own way,
however, for the political instability of the period led to a civil
war between 1341 and 1347. His opponents (who were largely
also the enemies of Katakouzenos and wanted to damage the
latter's cause by excommunicating Gregory) had gained a
power base in Constantinople and Thessalonike. They delated
Palamas for heresy, in 1344. The council of 1347 (called after
the civil war when Katakouzenos was emperor) had high on
its agenda the rehabilitation of Gregory and the doctrine for
which he had fought. He was rewarded for his labours with
consecration to the episcopal see of Thessalonike. A year or so
before the final 'Palamite' council was called in 1351, Gregory
issued a synopsis of his theology in a book now called *One
Hundred and Fifty Chapters*. He died at Thessalonike on 14
November 1359, and was canonised soon afterwards, merely
nine years after his death. The tenor of his thinking was
regarded as so important, so archetypally instructive, for the

Byzantine world that his feast was not merely entered into the calendar as an individual orthodox hierarch, but even established as one of the greater liturgical observances for the Second Sunday of Lent, a place it still commands to this day.

Gregory argued in the *Triads* and the *One Hundred and Fifty Chapters* that the monastic hesychast practices were a summation of the whole purpose of Christian life. The goal was to purify the heart and enter so deeply into contemplation of God that one might be chosen as an elect disciple and, like the three apostles, be called up to see the divine light that shone around Christ on Thabor.[22] This divine light was the deifying contact of God with his creatures, the multiplicity of ways in which God sustained the whole creation in being. It was the uncreated grace of God immediately perceived by the mystic; and it was this grace that differentiated the disciple from all other material creation, and gave the potentiality for communion with the Godhead:

> This shining light and deifying energy of God, which deifies all who participate in it, constitutes divine grace, but is not the nature of God as such. By this I do not mean that the divine nature is separated from those who have grace . . . since the Divine Nature is present everywhere. What I mean is that it is unapproachable, for no created thing can participate in the divine nature as such, as we have already demonstrated . . . Just as a face cannot be reflected by any material, only by such materials possessed of translucent smoothness, so too the energy of the Spirit cannot be found in all souls, only in those innocent of all perversity and crookedness.[23]

Gregory insists that the Light of Christ was not an attribute of God or a phenomenal form through which God chose to reveal himself (the appearance of an epiphany); on the contrary it was the unmediated presence of God himself. Gregory defined it as the Uncreated Energy.[24] It could thus be distinguished from the Essence of God, the divine nature itself, which was wholly unapproachable by creation, and absolutely unknowable in its infinite transcendence, both in this age and in the next. In the divine energy, however, the Godhead both created the world, and drew near to it in saving power. The incarnation was itself an act of the divine energy: here, that energy made the impossible, possible: that a man could simultaneously be God, and that human flesh could be assumed into personal union with the divine Logos. The incarnate Lord is therefore the supreme paradigm of how God is present to the Church[25] by virtue of his deifying energy. For Palamas, it was this same energy, the light of God, which was shown to the disciples on Thabor, and which illuminated them at a far deeper level than mere biological sight. The contact with God's Energy, in its highest form in the light of Thabor is, therefore, a direct encounter with God's powerful and salvific presence. Palamas suggests that after the giving of the eucharistic mysteries to the Church, disciples could even look for a more intimate communion with Christ by means of the divine light:

> The son of God, motivated by his incomparable love for humankind, did not just unite his divine hypostasis with our nature (clothing himself in a living body and an intelligent soul) but also united himself with human hypostases themselves, by mingling himself with each of the faithful through communion with his holy body. So he becomes one single body with us (Eph. 3:6) and transforms us into a temple of the undivided deity, because the very fullness of the godhead dwells bodily in Christ.[26] Then does it not follow that he will illuminate those who have a worthy communion with the divine ray of his body which is within us, radiating their souls, just as he illuminated the bodies of the disciples on Thabor?[27] On that day of the Transfiguration his body, the source of the very light of grace, had not yet been united with our bodies; and so illuminated externally those who were worthy enough to be near to it, and sent the radiance into their souls by the medium of their physical eyes. But now, for us, because it is mingled

with us, and co-exists within us, it surely illuminates the soul from within.[28]

The Energies of God are present throughout the creation, and disciples are able to participate in them by means of grace.[29] By his distinction of the Energy and the Essence, Palamas was able to explain how the Unknowable God could be the selfsame who entered into intimate relation with his Church. The Energy was not inferior to the Essence, for in God's simplicity no such distinction could be allowed[30] and by entering into connection with God's very Energy, the disciple came to participate directly in God himself. Thus the Unknowable became profoundly known, even as it remained ultimately Unknowable. The light that shone from Christ on Thabor, was the light of the divine glory. It is this light which the saints can see even here on earth, and which is the foretaste of the glory which will be the saints' admission into fuller participation with God in the next age:

> The Lord appeared on the mountain, as John Chrysostom says, more radiant than himself since the godhead had revealed its rays. His divine and ineffable light is God's Deity, and his Kingdom; it is the beauty and radiance of the divine nature; the vision and delight of the saints in the age that is without end; the natural radiance and glory of the godhead.[31]

Even in this age, the hesychast is drawn on through prayer, into an ever-deepening understanding through initiation into spiritual mysteries that transcend earthly limitations. Gregory seems to be exegeting the psalm text: 'In your light, we shall see light' (Ps. 36:9):

> Such a disciple will no longer see by sense-perception, but their vision will still be as clear, or even clearer than that by which the sight can perceive sensory objects. Such a disciple will see by going out of himself, for through the mysterious sweetness of this vision he will be taken in

rapture beyond all objects, all objective thought, and even beyond himself.[32]

Gregory's refined theological defence of the Hesychasts in the fourteenth century marked the definitive triumph of this spiritual school in all the churches of the Byzantine world. His radiant symbol of illuminated transfiguration became the organising idea of a whole nexus of spiritual teachers who had preceded him. In his hands the physical methods of prayer, advocated by Nikephoros of Athos, and the centrality of the Jesus Prayer as advocated by Gregory of Sinai, were joined with the lyrical and passionate mysticism of Symeon the New Theologian, and the heart-centred spirituality of Makarios and the desert tradition. Given his own genius for theological systematic that subordinated the whole discourse to experiential knowledge of God in prayer, Gregory Palamas should be regarded less as the founder of Hesychasm, and more as one of the supreme synthesisers of a variety of profound spiritual currents of the Eastern Church that came into flower in this period. It is no accident that the formation of this great spiritual synthesis led in turn to an immense renaissance of Byzantine iconography and culture in the Paleologan period that followed. This last renaissance of the Byzantine world before it fell to Islamic force of arms, produced masterpieces of Hesychast art that have never been equalled in subsequent eastern Christian civilisation, even when it remained free from external tyranny, such as in imperial Russia. The Hesychast culture of the monasteries of Athos, Russia, Serbia and Romania deepened in the centuries afterwards, under the harsh yoke of political oppression that was to come for most of the East Christian world, and gave Orthodox Christianity that mystical colouring that allowed it to survive, and which still decidedly marks it today.

8. 'THOUGH THERE STAND AROUND YOU TENS OF THOUSANDS OF ANGELS': THE SYMBOLIC WORLD OF EASTERN LITURGICAL PRAYER

WE CAN NEVER FORGET THAT BEAUTY

The establishment of Christianity in old Rus,[1] just over a thousand years ago in the time of Prince Vladimir of Kiev, produced a story which, though certainly retrospective and possibly legendary, sums up well the character of the eastern Christian liturgies of the Byzantine family. Vladimir, looking around for a religion to suit his people, is said to have sent delegates out to investigate various possibilities. When the entourage reached Constantinople and were taken into the church of Hagia Sophia to see the Byzantine emperor attending the eucharistic liturgy, they were overwhelmed by the glorious surroundings. The imperial choir was singing rich *a cappella*[2] syncopated responses, and the bishops, priests, and deacons in cloth of gold, chanted the mystical prayers while rose-scented incense billowed up in clouds to heaven above a sea of flickering candles under scintillating gold mosaics of the saints. It is recorded in the annals of the church historians, the *Russian Primary Chronicle*, that the delegates subsequently made their report back to Prince Vladimir:

> 'We knew not whether we were in heaven or still upon earth, for surely there is no such splendour or beauty anywhere upon the earth. We cannot describe it to you. Only this we know: that God dwells there among men,

and that their service surpasses the worship of all other
places. For we can never forget that beauty.'

The text above has often been used by the Orthodox trying to
connote something of their sense of the liturgical tradition of
prayer to those whose own traditions often have little in them
that could serve as a basis for comparison. The overwhelming
tenor of western Christian liturgies, including those of the
Catholic Church after the Second Vatican Council, is marked
by simple and clean lines, and a concomitant stress on clarity
and pedagogy. The services are short (usually less than an
hour) and predominantly concerned with direct communi-
cation: whether that is reading scriptural texts, or exegeting
them in discourses of one form or another, or allowing the
congregation to be involved in the sense of every word spoken
on their behalf by the celebrating minister. It was (and
remains) otherwise in the Byzantine Church. The pattern of
liturgical prayer, as it was established in Constantinople from
its ancient Syrian roots by the fourth century, and coming to
a more or less definitive form after the ninth, always laid a
great premium on the ethos of the divine mystery, and the
priority of God's action in the coming together of earth and
heaven in the celebration of the divine Eucharist. The Byzantine liturgy, accordingly, was a long solemn affair where the
divine drama unfurled in the supposition that all the men and
women present were players in a scene where Christ and the
angels were the primary actors, and where the descending
Spirit of God consecrated the gifts on the altar, but also moved
the minds and hearts and bodies of those present, to a symphonic awareness of the profound mysteries that were
symbolically taking place around them, through them, and in
them. In the Eastern Church liturgies, therefore, the body is
as much involved as the mind, and so although there are
certainly many readings and prayers of high theological
content, the intellectual aspect is never given precedence over
the whole complex of senses and levels of consciousness that
comprise the manifold living person. Often visitors will come

to an ordinary parish church of the Byzantine tradition looking to experience some of that hieratic splendour spoken of in the *Primary Chronicle*, only to find (and particularly so in the western diaspora of Orthodox Christianity) a small congregation, and an aged cantor who can hardly keep the note, and a poor and ill-decorated church building.

Those seeking aesthetic delight will often find consternation instead, but even where the church is poor and struggling there remains an abiding sense of the divine majesty given in the mysterious and sacred rituals that are common to all the Eastern Churches. In a sacred liturgy where the character of the clergy, or the singers, is not a predominantly important factor, but more so the evocation of the correct context for witnessing the divine descent, one often experiences a liberation that more pedagogically-directed church services do not allow. Only on few occasions does an Orthodox congregation all do the same thing: reverence the altar at the high moments. Otherwise the congregation seems often to be milling around, looking at various icons, and praying in different places in the church, and in different forms. There is a freedom in a tradition of worship that presumes the faithful will stand to pray (and so does not provide pews in church), a freedom to 'wander in the Lord' both bodily and intellectually, that the more formal western church pews and responsorial services do not allow.

THE SANCTIFICATION OF TIME AND ITS ELISION

During the course of the liturgy (particularly in Lent) the eastern rites will require numerous prostrations (*metanies*), where the clergy and faithful will often bend down their heads to touch the ground in worship, and in everyday services the people will constantly make the sign of the cross over themselves and bow from the waist at special parts of the service, or whenever the words have particularly touched them as 'a grace'. The bodily senses are further embraced as on numerous occasions the clergy send up clouds of sweet-smelling incense to prepare for the especially solemn parts of the liturgy. The offering of incense marks the particular consecration of time and place in a liturgy which is consciously designed to present the eschatological mystery of Christ's resurrection, which can never be limited to time or place. This is why, although the Divine Office in the Eastern Church (the services of the 'Hours' comprised of psalms, canticles and prayers) follows the idea of sanctifying the various times of the day, the liturgy proper, that is the Eucharist, is never associated with any sense of trying to sanctify time. It is, instead, the entrance into the Next Age where human history has already been consecrated in the once-for-all mystery of the cross and resurrection of the Saviour. It is, in the understanding of the Byzantine Church, an eschatological event, where time stands still, as it has been summoned into the presence of the eternal. The long stately progress of the service deliberately attempts to evoke that mystery of the eschatological salvation Christ has already won. Prayer is continually, and repetitively, offered until the hearts and minds of the believers are so steeped in the idea of the eschatological presence of God that the consecration of the gifts of bread and wine, by the coming down of the Spirit, seems a natural entry of the divine into the expectant dimension of the Church exiled in the world. Communion, something that is approached with great solemnity, and only after much fasting and individual preparation (often involving confession), is such a special occasion that many Orthodox faithful will plan to receive communion only four or five times a year. Infants and children, however, communicate at every liturgy, and there is also a contemporary 'liturgical movement' presently underway among the Orthodox attempting to make communion a more regular part of adult church attendance. For those who have fasted from all food and water from the day beforehand, sometimes fasted for several days beforehand, there is a deep significance in receiving the Eucharist, the taste of heavy leavened bread and sweet dark wine that breaks the hunger and refreshes mind and heart and body simultaneously. Several of the great ascetic priests of the Byzantine tradition fasted and liturgically celebrated so regularly that they came in the end to subsist entirely on the eucharistic gifts, which is physically quite possible, for they are a substantial food in and of themselves, and the act of the common taking of the mysteries gives the faithful a real sense of having shared a meal together. In many Orthodox churches, the communicants will remain at the east end of the church for several minutes after communicating, drinking a small cup of sweet wine together to break their fast, in a ritual reminiscent of the *Agape* (Love Feast) of the primitive Church.

PRAYERS OF THE LITURGY

The prayers that comprise the Byzantine liturgy represent the elevated thinking of Greek patristic theology in its heyday. The liturgy in common use is attributed to St John Chrysostom, the early fifth-century Archbishop of Constantinople, who organised the liturgy of the 'Great Church' of his capital city. It was this liturgy that became the archetype for most of the Churches that looked to Constantinople as their 'motherchurch'.[3] Today that includes all the Greek, Russian, Romanian, Bulgarian and other Slavic Churches who are bound together through this liturgical communion. Other liturgies are used on certain occasions in the church year, such as the *Liturgy of St James the Brother of the Lord* (the rite of the church of Jerusalem) and more often (in Lent) the *Liturgy of St Basil the Great*. The Byzantine rite has also had a large historical impact on the Coptic and the Oriental Orthodox Churches (the Non-Chalcedonian Churches) as well as the Armenians.

The liturgy is punctuated by regular intercessions.[4] Typically the deacon will come out from the altar area and stand before the icon screen with the faithful to intone the long series of intercessions which the church intends to raise formally to God in the time of the liturgy. To each of the prayers, sung in a slow solemn bass voice, the choir responds with the *Kyrie Eleison* or the *Gospodi Pomilui* (Lord, have mercy). The following example is called the *Litany of Fervent Intercession*:

Let us say with our whole soul and with our whole mind, let us say:

Lord, have mercy.

O Lord Almighty, God of our Fathers, we pray you, hear us and have mercy.

Lord, have mercy.

Have mercy on us, O God, according to your great mercy, we pray you, hear us and have mercy.

Lord, have mercy, Lord, have mercy, Lord, have mercy.

Again we pray for our most blessed Archbishop (N), and for all our brothers and sisters in Christ.

Lord, have mercy, Lord, have mercy, Lord, have mercy.

Again we pray for our god-fearing Rulers, their palace, and those in authority over us, and for the Christ-loving armed forces.

Lord, have mercy, Lord, have mercy, Lord, have mercy.

Again we pray for our brethren, the priests, deacons, monks and nuns, and for all our brothers and sisters in Christ.

Lord, have mercy, Lord, have mercy, Lord, have mercy.

Again we pray for the blessed and ever-remembered founders of this holy place; for our fathers and mothers, our brothers and sisters, the orthodox departed this life before us, who here and in all the world lie asleep in the Lord.

Lord, have mercy, Lord, have mercy, Lord, have mercy.

Again we pray for mercy, life, peace, health, salvation, visitation, forgiveness and remission of the sins of the servants of God: founders, benefactors, and supporters of this holy community.

Lord, have mercy, Lord, have mercy, Lord, have mercy.

Again we pray for those who bear fruit and do good works in this holy and all-venerable church; for those who serve, and those who sing, and for all the people here present, awaiting your great and rich mercy.

Lord, have mercy, Lord, have mercy, Lord, have mercy.

(Priest – silently)

O Lord our God, receive this fervent supplication of your servants, and have mercy upon us according to the multitude of your mercy, and send down upon us your compassions and upon all your people who await your great and rich mercy.

(Aloud – making the sign of the cross)

For you are a merciful God, who loves all humankind, and to you we offer glory:

✠ To the Father, and to the Son, and to the Holy Spirit, now and ever and to the Ages of Ages.

(Choir) Amen.

As the time for the readings of the divine Scriptures draws near there is the singing of a solemn hymn called the Trisagion (the Thrice-Holy). It is a short text but sung solemnly and slowly it marks a significant point in the movement of the liturgy, as if it were defining a sacred 'moment of attention'. The priest bends over the altar and while the choir is singing canticles for the day, he says the Trisagion prayer very quietly:

O Holy God, you are at rest in your holy place, hymned by the Seraphim with the thrice holy song [cf. Isa. 6:3], and glorified by the Cherubim, and worshipped by every heavenly power. From non-existence you brought the universe into being, and made male and female, according to your own image and likeness, adorning us with every gift of your grace. To those who ask, you give wisdom and understanding, and do not reject the sinner, but rather have established repentance for our salvation. You have counted us, your humble and unworthy servants, worthy to stand before the glory of your holy altar at this time, and to offer you due worship and praise. Accept, Master, even from the mouths of us sinners, the Thrice Holy Hymn, and visit us in your goodness. Pardon us every offence, both voluntary and involuntary. Sanctify our souls and bodies, and allow us to worship you in holiness all the days of our life; by the prayers of the holy Mother of

God, and of all the saints, who have been pleasing to you
in every age.
(*Aloud*)
For holy are you, our God, and to you we give glory:
✠ To the Father, and to the Son, and to the Holy Spirit.
Now and forever, and to the Ages of Ages.
(*Choir*): Amen.
(*At each stanza the congregation makes the sign of the
cross and bows down low*)
✠ Holy God, Holy Mighty, Holy Immortal, have mercy on
us.
✠ Holy God, Holy Mighty, Holy Immortal, have mercy on
us.
✠ Holy God, Holy Mighty, Holy Immortal, have mercy on
us.

THE HOLY ANAPHORA

The central prayer of consecration is called the *Anaphora*[5] of
the liturgy. It corresponds to the Latin rite 'Canon' of the Mass.
It too begins with a call from the deacon for the congregation
to stand to attention: 'Let us stand in awe, let us stand with
fear. Let us give our attention that we may offer the holy
oblation in peace!' And as the choir sings a responsorial the
priest silently continues with the opening prayer of 'eucharistic' thanksgiving to God:

It is right and fitting to hymn you, to bless you, to praise
you, to give thanks to you and to worship you in every
place of your dominion, for you are God ineffable, incon-
ceivable, invisible, incomprehensible, ever-existing, and
eternally the same: You and your Only Begotten Son,
and your Holy Spirit. You it was who brought us from
non-existence into being, and when we had fallen away,
raised us up again, never ceasing to do all things until
you had brought us up to heaven and endowed us with
your kingdom which is to come. For all these things we

give thanks to you, and to your Only Begotten Son, and your Holy Spirit; for all things of which we know, and of which we know not, and for all the benefits bestowed upon us, both manifest and unseen. And we give thanks to you also for this liturgy which you have deigned to receive at our hands, even though there stand beside you thousands of archangels, and tens of thousands of angels, the cherubim and the seraphim, six-winged, many-eyed, soaring aloft, borne upon their wings:
(The priest sings out aloud while striking the sacred vessels on the altar to make them chime out simultaneously):
Singing, crying, shouting the triumphal hymn and saying:
(The choir sings) Holy, Holy, Holy, Lord of Sabaoth. Heaven and earth are full of your glory. Hosanna in the highest. Blessed is he who comes in the name of the Lord. Hosanna in the highest.

The Lord's words of institution, spoken over the bread and wine, are the same as in the western Church liturgies, but in the Byzantine rite the words of institution themselves are not regarded as the final consecration of the mysteries: this is accomplished rather by and at the descent of the Holy Spirit onto the altar which occurs shortly after, at the *Epiclesis* (The Invocation), when the priest prays this most sacred of prayers, bowed low over the altar:

Again we offer you this rational and bloodless worship, and we beseech you, and pray you, and supplicate you: send down your Holy Spirit upon us and upon these gifts here spread forth. And make this bread ✠ the precious body of your Christ [Amen]; and that which is in this cup ✠ the precious blood of your Christ [Amen]. Changing them by your Holy Spirit ✠ ✠ ✠.
[Amen. Amen. Amen.]

A long series of prayers for the Church 'who have preceded us' follows the consecration. All the prophets, apostles, evan-

gelists and martyrs are listed, asking that the Risen Christ
will remember them all in his glory, and ending with the prayer
that he would remember: 'especially our all-holy, immaculate,
most blessed and glorious Lady, the Mother of God and Ever-
Virgin Mary.' And then there follows a long series of prayers
for the Church still labouring on earth. In the Liturgy of St
Basil, this list comes to an end with the beautiful synopsis:

> Hope of the hopeless, Saviour of the storm-tossed,
> Safe Harbour of the voyager,
> Physician of the sick:
> Lord, be yourself 'all things to all',
> you who know every one of us, our prayers, our dwelling
> places, and all our needs.

The communion of the Mysteries, under both species, then
follows, for those who have prepared themselves to receive.
The congregation says together this prayer, so redolent of the
ancient Church and its strict discipline of 'guarding the liturgical secret' from catechumens and non-believers:

> Receive me this day, O Son of God,
> A communicant of your Mystic Supper;
> For I will not speak of your Mystery to your enemies,
> Nor, like Judas, will I give you a kiss,
> But like the thief I will confess you:
> Remember me, O Lord, in your Kingdom.

The eucharistic liturgy still unfolds in the Byzantine
Church, as it did many centuries ago, as a solemn and moving
ritual in which the closely harmonised singing of the *a capella*
choir alternates with the intonations of the bishop, or the
priest and deacon. It is possessed of a mystical and luminous
quality, but it is something that is far from facile, for even
the physical demands it makes upon worshippers who may
sometimes stand for several hours on end, have to be felt to
be appreciated, and the much repeated cycles of prayers and
intercessions are designed to call down the soul from its
incessant wanderings and impatience, and instil within it a

newly focused spiritual attentiveness (*prosoche*) to the advent of the Lord of Mysteries. This recalling from our meanderings is not always an easy discipline. Often it is a considerable struggle, in a world that gives a premium to speed, superficiality and quick answers, so to be summoned back to attentiveness over such a long period of prayer and spiritual communion.

Even so, the liturgy is generally regarded as a process, more than a set form of prayers demanding our intellectual assent, and the eucharistic transformation of the faithful is something expected to initiate a change that develops into a lifetime's fidelity. Even the Orthodox who do not regularly attend services during the year, will be found packing the churches to be present for Easter and Christmas celebrations, and their presence on these great festal occasions is far from a mere formalism; the intensity of such services when the larger diaspora gathers is quite palpable, and forms the occasion when many visitors gain their first impressions of the eastern spirit of worship.

BYZANTINE EVENING PRAYER

The other main forms of regular service in the Byzantine Church today are Vespers (known as *Esperinos* or Vigil), preceding the feast on the evening before, and *Orthros* or Day-Dawn service, corresponding to the western rite of Matins (Russian parish practice combines them on the evening before). There are the whole other range of monastic offices too, but these are generally kept only in monastic houses. Byzantium retained the Jewish liturgical custom of beginning the day with sunset and the lighting of the lamps of the home and the church. The Vesperal service is built around Old Testament readings and the symbolic lighting of the lamps of eventide.[6] It turns around the symbol of lamp-lighting, the offering of incense and the procession of the Gospel book. The service always commences with a blessing and common prayers (The Trisagion prayers[7]) and then the choir intones Psalm 103, the great prayer of the cosmos blessing God for the gifts of life and nurturing. While this is being chanted the priest stands on the steps in front of the iconostasis, and quietly recites a series of seven prayers of varying length for 'the lighting of the lamps' (*Lychnapsia* prayers), all of which culminate in a doxology – a giving of glory to the Holy Trinity. The following is a short example:

> You who are celebrated by the never-silent hymns and unceasing doxologies of the Holy Powers: fill our mouths with your praise that we may magnify your holy name. And give to us a share and inheritance along with all those who fear you in truth and keep your commandments: through the intercessions of the holy Mother of God, and of all your saints; ✠ for to you are due all glory, honour, and worship, to the Father, and to the Son, and to the Holy Spirit, now, and forever, and to the Ages of Ages, Amen.

There follow litanies and the sections of the Psalter appointed to be sung for that week. The normal cycle of Divine Office is governed by a pattern of eight tones (*Octoechos*) and the service book that contains them all lists the various proper responses for the day. The eight different tones are also different tonalities in the type of chant used for that week, ranging from a regular, slightly pulsing chant rhythm to the minor and more 'penitential' tonal voices. The system of Byzantine chant was from the outset flexible and much varied in its colourations, and the whole tradition of the music, both ecclesiastical and secular, is now undergoing a renaissance. The Slavic versions tended to simplify the complexities of Byzantine music, and such a simplification can also be seen in many modern parish services. The Slavic monastic chant is more easily adapted to English usage, and is probably the form that most observers to English language services in the Orthodox diaspora will experience: the closely harmonised and rhythmic singing of a small choir. On Saturday evening, the Vespers for Sunday, the psalm appointed is always Psalm 1.

After this the choir sings 'Lord, I have cried', either the full form of Psalm 140, or an abbreviated version:

> Lord, I have cried to you, hear my voice.
> Lord, I have cried to you, hear my voice.
> Attend to the sound of my prayer.
> Hear me when I call to you.
> Let my prayer come before you like incense.
> The raising of my hands like an evening oblation.

On the second to last line the priest, now in the altar area, begins to incense the sanctuary and the whole church. When the choir finishes with the responses for the day the priest circles the altar with the Book of the Gospels (or if it is not a feast that has its own Gospel reading, with the censer) and makes a procession back into the nave of the church to stand in front of the Royal Doors of the Iconostasis. The procession of the Gospel book symbolises the majestic and mystical advent of Christ into the world as Teacher and Illuminator. The procession with the censer symbolises the grace of the Spirit coming into the world and suffusing the experience of the church at prayer. At that time all the congregation sing the ancient 'lamplighting' hymn of Vespers, probably written in the early third century. It is called 'The Gladsome Light':

> Jesus Christ, The Gladdening Light
> of the Immortal Father's holy Glory;
> The Heavenly, Holy, Blessed One;
> As the Sun declines we see the light of evening,
> and sing our hymn to God, the Father, Son, and Holy
>   Spirit.
> Worthy are you, O Son of God,
> through each and every moment,
> that joyful songs should hymn you.
> You are the Giver of our Life, and so the world gives
>   glory.

Other songs and responsorial verses are chanted by the choir. On Saturday evenings, that is the Vespers for Sundays, they take as their theme the resurrection victory of Christ. The service draws to a conclusion with the 'Canticle of Simeon' ('Now, master, dismiss your servant in peace, according to your promise, for my eyes have seen your salvation'). As with the western service of Compline, there is a final hymn to the Virgin (*Theotokion*) and then the blessing and dismissal given by the priest.

If the Vespers is that of a particularly high feast, the service of *Litiya* and *Artoklasia* follows immediately. This is named after the 'breaking of bread' and is a form of the *Agape* or Love Feast that was maintained in the early Church. Canticles are chanted in honour of the saint being celebrated, or the Feast of the Lord, or of the Virgin Mary, and intercessions are made for the Church. Loaves of bread, and bottles of wine and olive oil, and a dish of boiled wheat are placed with icons and candles on a small table in the middle of the church. This is blessed with the following prayer:

> O Lord Jesus Christ Our God,
> Who blessed the five loaves in the wilderness
> And from them satisfied the five thousand,
> ✠ Yourself bless these loaves, this wheat, and this oil,
> And multiply them in this city, and throughout the world,
> And sanctify the faithful, who shall eat of them in faith.
> For you are the blessing and sanctification of all things,
> O Christ, our God,
> ✠ And to you we ascribe all glory,
> Together with your Unoriginate Father,
> And your All-Holy, Good, and Life-Giving Spirit:
> Now and forever, and to the Ages of Ages, Amen.

The bread is then broken and dipped in the wine and distributed for the congregation to eat and share with one another. Often portions are taken back to family members who have remained at home. At the end of the service the blessed oil is used to anoint the foreheads of those present in a prayer for blessing and healing.

THE GREAT AND GLORIOUS PASCHAL MYSTERIES

The abundance of other services in the Byzantine ritual is closely tied to the liturgical year, with its fixed cycle of Sundays and the moveable cycle of feasts dependent on Pascha,[8] the great festival of festivals around which the whole liturgical year basically revolves. The services of Great and Holy Week are especially solemn and expansive. The Church's fasting rules,[9] which apply throughout the year on Wednesdays and Fridays, are extended across all forty days of Great Lent (as well as the other lesser Lenten periods preceding the Feast of the Virgin's Falling Asleep on 15 August, the Holy Apostles in mid summer, and Christmas). The passion services repeat the theme extensively of the Bridegroom's Coming – the eschatological warning to the Church to keep awake, and keep watching, for the hour of the return is not known. The eschatological tone of the services, calling for continual repentance and renovation of heart from the faithful, is allied with the sense of providing the burial service for the suffering Christ. The Great Friday service of the *Epitaphios* carries the winding sheet of Christ around the church – often outside the church through the villages in Orthodox lands – while the chants of lamentation rise up in the 'plagal' or minor mode of Church music. In Greece and Russia it is common to see old and young people weeping unrestrainedly as they join together their annual mourning of the passion and death of Christ with the lamentation of all their departed kin. The sense of sorrow turns to luminous joy on the Paschal service of midnight on the Day of Resurrection.

A short time before midnight on Great Saturday, the last verses lamenting the passion of Christ are sung, and the icon of the entombed Christ, the *Epitaphios*, is censed and carried back into the altar area by the priest. As midnight falls in a wholly darkened church, the celebrating priest strikes a new fire, and lights the Paschal candle. Carrying it round the altar, the clergy in the sanctuary behind the iconostasis light their own candles from it, and a glimmer of light begins to spread.

Standing in the Royal Doors facing the people the priest slowly chants over and again the refrain:

> Come ye. Take light from the Light that is never overtaken by the night. Come and glorify Christ who has risen from the dead!

And the whole body of people come up to light their candles from the one flame. When the church is a flickering sea of fire, the great golden Book of the Gospels is taken with the Paschal candle and all the icons and banners from the church, and all process outside to the constant slow repetition of the solemn chant:

> The angels in heaven hymn your resurrection, O Christ Saviour. Make us also, who are on the earth, worthy to glorify you with a pure heart.

The procession turns and comes back before the doors of the church, now closed and sealed, to represent the tomb of Jesus. There the Paschal gospel is proclaimed, and for the first of many times to follow that night, and in the weeks to come, the Paschal Hymn bursts out in triumph from the choir and the collected faithful:

> Christ is risen from the dead, trampling death by death,
> And to those in the tombs bestowing life!

This is the moment when the congregation enters once more to find the church fully illuminated, and the Nine Odes of the Paschal Canon are sung while all the church bells are rung, and every lamp that can be lit is made to make the church as brightly radiant as possible. At regular intervals during the singing of the Great Canon the priest comes to the centre of the altar step and shouts out, 'Christ is risen!' All the people shout back each time: 'He is risen indeed!' This becomes the standard way the Orthodox greet one another for the rest of Bright Week that follows. The solemn kiss of peace is also given, the threefold kiss on the left, the right, and the left cheek again. The Russian priest Sergius Bulgakov (1871–1944) eloquently described the emotions attendant on this festival:

> All the services pale before the beauty of the grandiose rites of Lent, and above all of Holy Week. And the luminaries themselves pale, as stars of the night before the light of the rising sun, before the light and joy of the night of Easter. The resurrection of Christ is a high festival in the whole Christian world, but nowhere is it so luminous as in Orthodoxy.[10]

Apart from the great cycle of the liturgy, the Byzantine tradition stresses the importance of daily prayer as a regular preparation of the spirit to be able to participate as 'one awake' in the sacred liturgy. The custom of the Jesus Prayer is commonly advocated. A person will stand at home before the icons which every Orthodox household has placed in some corner, and using a small woollen rope of a hundred knots, repeats slowly, time and time again, the prayer of the penitent tax collector held up by the Lord as a paradigm of salvation: 'Lord Jesus Christ, Son of God, have mercy on me a sinner.' There are numerous other occasions when a priest might be invited to the house to provide blessings or prayers for the sick and the dying, but the tradition of private prayer is also strong, and several varieties of Prayer Books are commonly available.[11] In Orthodox households many prayers are taught to the young and so remain 'known by heart' throughout a person's life. Apart from the Lord's Prayer and the Creed, these are a few examples of the common prayers of the Byzantine tradition. The prayer 'Heavenly King' begins most things:

> O Heavenly King the Paraclete, the Spirit of Truth who are present everywhere, filling all things, Treasury of Good, and Giver of Life, come and dwell in us and cleanse us of every stain, and save our souls, O Good One.

And of two of the most frequently used prayers to the Virgin, one is a song of praise:

More Honourable than the Cherubim,
And beyond compare more glorious than the Seraphim,
For incorruptibly you gave birth to God the Word:
Truly Mother of God we magnify you.

And the other a prayer for her maternal intercession:

Open to us the gates of your compassion, O Blessed Mother of God. In that we have placed our hope in you may we never be confounded. Through you may we be delivered from all adversity; for you are the deliverance of the race of Christians.

Daily morning devotions often consist of Psalm 120 and include the following prayer:

We bless you, Most High God and Lord of Mercy, who are always doing great and inscrutable things with us, glorious and wonderful and without number. You grant us sleep for rest from our infirmities and repose from the burdens of our much toiling flesh. We thank you for you have not let us be destroyed in our sins, but rather have given us your accustomed love, and though we had sunk into despair, you raised us up again to glorify your power. And so, we implore your incomparable goodness: enlighten the eyes of our comprehension and raise up our minds from the heavy sleep of indolence. Open our mouth and fill it with your praise, that we might be able, undistractedly, to sing and confess that you are God, glorified in all and by all, the Eternal Father, with your Only Begotten Son, and your All-Holy, Good, and Life-Giving Spirit. ✠ Now and forever, and to the Ages of Ages. Amen.

On Saturdays this prayer is replaced by the weekly commemoration of the dead:

Remember Lord, our fathers and mothers, brothers and sisters, who have fallen asleep in the hope of the resurrection to eternal life, and all those who ended this life in righteousness and faith. Pardon them every transgression which they committed, whether voluntary or involuntary, in word or in deed or in thought. Shelter them in places of light, in places of refreshment, in places of peace, whence every grief, sorrow, and lamentation has been banished, and where the light of your countenance shines on all your saints, of all ages, to gladden them. Grant to them your Kingdom and participation in your inexpressible and everlasting blessings, and the enjoyment of your life of unending blessedness. For you are the Life, the Resurrection, and the Repose of all your servants who have fallen asleep, Christ our God, ✠ and to you we give glory together with your Eternal Father, and your All-Holy, Good, and Life-Giving Spirit. Now and forever, and to the Ages of Ages. Amen.

And so it is that by a recurring cycle of liturgical celebrations and daily prayers, underlined by regular practices of fasting, and the customs of bowing, venerating the icons, and making frequent 'signs of the cross' during prayer, the Byzantine tradition fosters the abiding sense of Christ's sanctification of ordinary life. It is as if the life of prayer is an invocation, a state of readiness, in accordance with those words of the Lord: 'So I say it to all of you. Stay awake, for you know not the hour of the Bridegroom's coming' (Matt. 25:13).

9. AN EPILOGUE: THE SPIRITUAL CULTURE OF BYZANTINE CHRISTIANITY

THE SEARCH FOR THE BEAUTIFUL

Our ending becomes again our beginning: the beauty of Christ which shines through centuries of the Eastern Church's tradition of prayer, and art, and intellectual culture; a beauty that always renews itself however much it is degraded by outrageous failures or incapacities on the part of Christians. This beauty, and the sense of its healing qualities is, for me at least, the dominant motif of the entire Byzantine spiritual tradition. The 'Beauty ever ancient ever new', as Augustine described it in his *Confessions*, is no abstraction in the way in which the Church apprehends it, rather a powerful personal allurement, a sensing of the presence of God in all the awesomeness and holiness of what that means: and above all an admission into the divine presence, not an approach to it. For in this way Christian spirituality distinguishes itself from other kinds of 'spiritualities' which do not prioritise that fundamental truth, that: 'Unless the Lord build the house, in vain do the builders labour' (Ps. 127:1). It is this decisive experience that characterises eastern Christian spiritual awareness: that it is God who is the beginning and end of the revelation of all beauty in a human life, and God alone who calls the soul into the divine consciousness, forming and transfiguring the whole capacities of a human life in the process, rendering a human existence capable of being the translucent vehicle of a divine existence. As Athanasios of Alexandria (borrowing from

Irenaeus) once put it: 'For He became human, that we humans might become divine' (*De Incarnatione* 54.3).

The divine priority in salvation, as reiterated constantly by the Byzantine tradition, is not merely an affirmation of the absolute transcendence of the Saviour, but also a celebration of the manner in which God constantly stoops down (the divine *katabasis* of the economy of revelation and salvation) to greet fallen and broken creatures, and restore them time and time again to wholeness, and grace and, indeed, to overwhelming beauty. This is the Byzantine theology of *theosis*, the divinisation by grace which proximity to God affords the soul and body of the disciple. It is the dominant motif and recurring theme of all East Christian culture and tradition. The transfiguration of the individual person, human society, and the entire cosmos itself is the perennial goal of the God of salvation, and the constant invitation such a God of renewal offers to a spent world, and to an exhausted humanity.

A GOLDEN CHAIN OF LIVING SAINTS

Symeon the New Theologian characterised it in the form of a golden chain, whose links were the saints of one generation to the next, including his present time: all of whom articulated the inner tradition of the Church, by modelling it in their lives and attitudes. For Symeon, his spiritual father Symeon Eulabes had rescued him from years of wandering in the dark, by modelling for him the true Christian life, and passing on the love of Christ in the concrete form of a teacher who genuinely and open-heartedly loved his disciples, and wanted to form them in Christ. Symeon's point in positing this image of the golden chain was that the inner Christian tradition, its mystical tradition, its awareness of how the river of the divine Spirit courses through it across the centuries, can only be apprehended by experience (*aisthesis*) and never by mere reflection or theory. The Christian life, therefore, cannot be at base merely a metaphysical position, or a set of beliefs, or a habitual formalised behavioural posture. The Byzantine writers, Symeon chief among them, insist time and time again that Christianity is wholly a praxis, an experiment, a doing, a sensing. It is a journey that may be long or incredibly short to the radiant vision of God, depending on God's dialectic with the soul. But the very setting out on the journey renders the individual immediately in the presence of fellow-travellers who are themselves already radiant in the Spirit, and who point to the even more radiant presence of the Light of the World who accompanies all such travellers. In other words, Symeon's point about the golden chain whose links were the saints in each generation, was that the Christian experience cannot so much be learned, as needs to be 'caught', from person to person, and only from one radiant heart to another heart which thus begins to see. Faith and love in Christ are transmitted only in this manner, from one candle to another. The Byzantine spiritual tradition is, therefore, very much a communal ecclesial affair, not a solipsistic mysticism that refuses to test itself against the harsh realities of the world and its pain, but one that resists all bureaucratic stultification by its constant appeal to praxis and experience. Only those who have known, and seen and touched, can stand as authentic guides. Their writings are offered as testimonies of what has been experienced, what can be experienced now, and as such they all have a directly appealing quality. Despite their historical limitations and their dialectical blind spots, they retain a surprising freshness, still applicable in a world where though few are monks or nuns, all are still challenged by the selfsame Gospel injunction to 'Seek first the Kingdom of Heaven' (Matt. 6:33).

In the diaspora of eastern Christianity that has happened within the twentieth century, through mass migration of traditionally 'eastern' European peoples, the Orthodox Byzantine tradition has come to be more and more a familiar presence in the western Christian world. The writers who have always formed the mainspring of its spirituality and praxis are only now emerging to inform a more universalised Christian consciousness, in an age of immensely powerful mass media. These ancient writers are, ironically, probably enjoying in this strange diaspora their greatest exposure ever in the history of the Church. Perhaps they are to enjoy their greatest era of influence no longer in their own time, and geographical or cultural heartlands, but in a brave new world where the Church stands as much as ever in need of consolidation, courage, and coherence.

BEAUTY AND COMMUNION

The Byzantine saints, and the Eastern Church's deep grounding in a theology of endurance, a theology of beauty and hopefulness, it can only be hoped, will have much to say for seekers after the beauty of the Risen Lord, even in this time. Such an opening out to other Christians of the richness of the eastern tradition is the deepest level of ecumenical gift possible, far greater in importance than any formal ecumenical dialogue. The principle adopted at the fifteenth-century Council of Florence, when the Latins and Byzantines were desperately seeking ways forward in ecumenical rapprochement before Islamic power finally rode over Byzantium in a tidal wave, is one that still has an enduring significance: 'Saints cannot differ in faith.' The disciple recognises the heart of the Church's experience across the ages in the writings of its saints and, in the features of the saints who have been formed in the image of Christ, it sees no less than the beauty of the Lord, and is called out to participate in it personally.

I hope that this small book of introduction to the Byzantine tradition may serve such an ecumenical purpose, and perhaps more than that, that it might even function as a small window onto the real substance of what the Church's spiritual tradition is essentially about: the deifying encounter with the Lord of Glory, manifestly different for every individual according to their own condition and state, but always 'the same yesterday and today' (Heb. 13:8) in that it is the same Spirit of Christ who illuminates the Church of every generation – a restless and mysterious dynamic of the resurrection presence that seeks with each generation to raise up saints who will continue the witness of the resurrection grace of their Lord.

A SHORT EPILOGUE

We have left behind the twentieth century, one of the bloodiest ever known in the history of humankind, and one in which technological advances have gone forward at a dizzying pace equally unprecedented in the history of the world – an era where great benefits have been promised and offered, but have at many instances also left the planet itself gasping for breath in the wake of the despoliation and defilement of the very springs of our existence and our earth. At such a time, and in such a *kairos* (that poised moment of grace in which raw history becomes the material of encounter with the God of salvation) the relearning of the discipline, the attentiveness, and the quiet beauty of what Christ has to say to his faithful – and what the Spirit wishes to write in the secret of the heart – has never been so relevant, or so necessary, or so urgent.

NOTES

CHAPTER 1. PRELUDE

1. Byzantium was the name of the city in its first foundation as a Greek colony on the Bosphorus. Constantine the Great refounded it as the new capital of the Roman Empire, intending it to be from the outset a Christian city. It was renamed Constantinople (modern Istanbul) but still retained the old title, which today has come to signify the wider cultural aspects of the whole complex of East Christian civilisation. Cf. J.A. McGuckin, 'Constantinople', in A. Hastings (ed.), *The Oxford Companion to Christian Thought* (Oxford, 2000).
2. Not least the Christian holy places of Israel which were built by the Byzantines, the papal palaces and basilicas of Rome which were given by Constantine for church use, or the ancient monasteries of Sinai, Greece, Russia, Serbia and Romania.
3. For a good overview see J. Pelikan, *The Spirit of Eastern Christendom* (Chicago, 1974), or J. Meyendorff, *Imperial Unity and Christian Divisions* (New York, 1989).
4. Cf. D.M. Nicol. *Immortal Emperor: The Life and Legend of Constantine Palaiologus, Last Emperor of the Romans* (Cambridge and New York, 1992).
5. See G. Florovsky, *The Eastern Fathers of the Fourth Century*, vol. 7 of the Collected Works (Vaduz/Belmont MA, 1987).
6. Cf. A. Bryer and M. Cunningham (eds.), *Mount Athos and Byzantine Monasticism* (Aldershot, 1996).
7. Cf. S. Joanta, *Romania: Its Hesychast Tradition* (Wildwood, 1992).

CHAPTER 2. THE BEAUTY OF GOD

1. A title by which he wanted to evoke the Byzantine idea of the 'Fool for Christ': that is, the saint whose wholehearted dedication to the Gospel maxims led him or her into such a dislocation from contemporary culture that they were regarded as 'idiots' by their peers.
2. R.J. O'Connell, 'Eros and Philia in Plato's Moral Cosmos', in *NeoPlatonism in Early Christian Thought*, ed. H. Blumenthal and R.A. Markus (London, 1981), pp. 3–19.

3. In more or less the same way as it could be commonly agreed that a 'good' vase or a 'good' horse meant simply one of these things that was at one and the same time an elegant as well as an efficient specimen.

4. i.e. by Noetic intuition, beyond aesthetic or sensory experience. For a comment on this passage cf. J. Adam, *The Religious Teachers of Greece* (Edinburgh, 1908), pp. 390–7 – Gifford Lectures 1904–6.

5. Text from *The Symposium,* tr. B. Jowett and ed. R.M. Hare and D.A. Russell (London, 1970), pp. 224–5 (slightly adapted).

6. *Nous* in Platonic thought was the spiritual identity of the essential Soul (the pre-existing and eternal consciousness). In Christian thought the term was semantically modified to signify the 'spiritual intelligence' of the body-soul composite which is the human creature.

7. Cf. J.A. McGuckin, 'Florovsky', in A. Hastings (ed.), *The Oxford Companion to Christian Thought* (Oxford, 2000).

8. At the beginning of the twentieth century, Harnack popularised the view of Church history as a progressive 'Hellenisation of Christianity', citing Gnosticism as the chief example of decline from biblical simplicity. Recent scholarship has supported Florovsky's scepticism as to whether the two ideas can be so discretely treated, and whether biblical thought is so separate from the Greek culture in which the gospel appeared.

9. *Theosis* means 'deification by grace'. It is the East Christian corresponding notion to the Latin concept of salvation by grace; but it was more 'ontologically' grounded: that is, it conceived the dynamic of salvation of the human race as having been effected by the Divinity's personal adoption of human nature. In this divine act of incarnation something substantive was felt to have happened to the human nature itself. What was impossible (the flesh of humankind being capable of sustaining the divine presence) was now seen to have been made possible in Christ. What happened in his case (the incarnation of God) as a 'natural' reality (in so far as it happened in and around his divine and human natures) was posited by the eastern fathers as a mystical 'grace' for the Church. The disciples were thus destined in and from the incarnation to be transfigured into the God-Man: mystically incorporated in Christ. This was partially accomplished through the Eucharist, but seen to be finally perfected when human nature itself was thoroughly transfigured into the state of the 'glorious body' in the Next Age. Cf. J.A. McGuckin, 'Deification', in A. Hastings (ed.), *The Oxford Companion to Christian Thought.* See also idem, *The Transfiguration of Christ in Scripture and Tradition* (New York, 1984).

10. Cf. J.A. McGuckin, *St Cyril of Alexandria: The Christological Controversy* (Brill, Leiden, 1994); idem, *Cyril of Alexandria: On the Unity of Christ* (New York, 1995).

11. Maximos Confessor, *1st Century on Theology,* 84–5.

12. The pre-Christian (and later Christian) Greek ideal of the Good and the Beautiful in harmony: the standard of a moral and cultured civilised existence.

13. The self-emptying mentioned in Philippians 2:7.

14. Dionysios the Pseudo-Areopagite: *On the Divine Names* 4.14.

15. Maximos Confessor, *Fifth Century of Various Texts*, 83–6 passim.

16. The great Catholic theologian, Hans Urs von Balthasar, in his monumental work *The Glory of the Lord* (7 vols, ET Edinburgh, 1982), saw the necessity of elaborating such a 'theological aesthetics'.

17. A proto-catechesis – based upon notions that are familiar to the world, in language it recognises, so that contemporary culture can be taken to the higher and deeper signification of the true mysteries and values it has already partially recognised, partially preserved, which the gospel wishes to purify.

CHAPTER 3. AN IMAGELESS VISION

1. Our historical information about Evagrios comes from Palladius' *Lausiac History* by C. Butler (ET Cambridge, 1904), pp. 116–123, and from the *Church Histories* of Socrates (H.E. 4.23) and Sozomen (H.E. 6.30).

2. The *Five Theological Orations*, Nos. 27–31 in Gregory's corpus.

3. Chapter 38 of Palladius' *Lausiac History* is devoted to Evagrios.

4. *Apophthegmata Patrum*, Evagrios 7 (PG. 65. 176A); Arsenios 5 (PG. 65. 88D–89A); Euprepios 7 (PG. 65. 172D).

5. Origen envisaged the creation as originally entirely spiritual – the angelic circle around the divine Logos, all in pure harmony. Spiritual inattentiveness caused some of the spirits to fall away from the inner circle and so division and disharmony was caused. Eventually the decline of the lapsed spirit/souls was so marked, and their status so ontologically decadent, that they declined into materialised forms, for which God prepared a material creation for their correction and (eventually chastened) return to the spiritual domain. The logic of this doctrine of the pre-cosmic fall, was that we who now live on earth were once the pre-existent spirits in close communion with the divine Logos, and thus in perfect beatitude. Our spiritual ascent is synonymous with our salvific return to the Logos, both for Origen and Evagrios. By the time of Evagrios, however, this 'Origenistic' attitude to spiritual cosmology was becoming more and more a matter of theological conflict in the desert.

6. 'The body is the friend of the soul.' The text can be found as fragment 12.13 in *Evagriana Syriaca* (Louvain, 1952).

7. cf. E.A. Clark, *The Origenist Controversy* (Princeton, 1992).

8. Monologistic prayer was the long-drawn-out repetition of a few simple words or biblical phrases (the Jesus Prayer is a prime example) which became mantra-like ways of focusing the spiritual intellect and

preventing it from wandering, and was much used in the Egyptian desert monasteries. See I. Hausherr, *The Name of Jesus* (Kalamazoo, 1978).

9. *Short Teaching on Asceticism and Quietness, Philokalia*, vol. 1, p. 31.
10. *Praktikos* 6–14.
11. *Chapters on Prayer* 50.
12. *Praktikos* 15.
13. *ibid.* 1.
14. John Cassian translated Evagrios' word *apatheia* into Latin as *puritas cordis*: clarity of heart, as in Jesus' commendation in Matthew 5:8.
15. *Short Teaching on Asceticism and Quietness, Philokalia*, vol. 1, p. 32.
16. *Texts on Discrimination, Philokalia*, vol. 1, p. 39.
17. *Chapters on Prayer* 14.
18. *Praktikos* 42.
19. *On Discrimination, Philokalia*, vol. 1, p. 46.
20. *Chapters on Prayer* 35.
21. *Praktikos* 63–5.
22. *Chapters on Prayer* 69; *Praktikos* 114–120, 128, 142, 152.
23. *Chapters on Prayer* 3.
24. *ibid.* 52.
25. *ibid.* 71.
26. *ibid.* 4.
27. *ibid.* 5.
28. *ibid.* 6.
29. *ibid.* 9.
30. *ibid.* 11.
31. *ibid.* 43.
32. *ibid.* 32.
33. *ibid.* 62.
34. *ibid.* 80–1.
35. *ibid.* 74–5.
36. *ibid.* 82.
37. *Ad Monachos* 116.
38. Translated by S. Brock, *The Syriac Fathers on Prayer and the Spiritual Life* (Kalamazoo, 1987), pp. 66–75.

CHAPTER 4. THE PRAYER OF THE HEART IN THE DESERT TRADITION

1. Men like Barsanuphios and John with their aphoristic maxims and morals, or the 'desert fathers' who appear in the collections of *Apophthegmata* (Sayings of the Desert Fathers) that were being assembled at this time.
2. cf. Mark 7:21; Matt. 12:34; John 12:40; Luke 1:51; Luke 2:35; Luke 9:47; Luke 24:25, 38, *et al.*

3. Sayings of the Desert Fathers, *Vitae Patrum* 5.1.11.
4. *Letters of Ammonas* 6.
5. *Ladder* 28.33–34.
6. *ibid.* 28.11.
7. *ibid.* 28.4–5. The single phrase was 'Lord, have mercy on me a sinner'.
8. The Jesus Prayer consists in the slow repetition of the words: Lord Jesus Christ, Son of God, have mercy on me a sinner. The physical rhythm of breathing was meant to be synchronised with the feeling of 'descent of the mind to the heart' as a device of gathering psychic attentiveness in the heart, readying the monk for the sense of the presence of God. It was a Niptic exercise (an exercise of penitent sorrow) that was meant to flower into the mystical awareness of the presence of God's love and mercy.
9. *On Spiritual Knowledge* 83.
10. *ibid.* 85.
11. *ibid.* 56–7.
12. *ibid.* 78.
13. *ibid.* 29.
14. *ibid.* 59.
15. *Homily* 42.3.
16. *ibid.* 43.7.
17. *ibid.* 43.1.
18. *ibid.* 43.2.
19. *ibid.* 43.3.
20. *ibid.* 43.3.
21. *ibid.* 43.6.
22. *ibid.* 43 6.
23. *ibid.* 15.20.
24. The eastern term for head of a monastery – or abbot.
25. *Discourse* 5.
26. *ibid.* 5.
27. *Maxims* 5.
28. *Reply to the Hermits*.
29. We shall come back to this important notion of the Jesus Prayer in the course of the chapter on Hesychasm, when the later Byzantine teachers refined it as the central method of a powerful school of mystical thought.
30. 'Heart speaks to heart' – the affairs of the heart can only be 'read' or spoken at that common level of encounter.

CHAPTER 5. GOD'S SINGERS

1. cf. A. di Nola, *The Prayers of Man* (London, 1962).
2. cf. J.A. McGuckin, *At the Lighting of the Lamps: Hymns from the Ancient Church* (Harrisburg, Pa., 1997).

3. The very word *textus* – the 'text' derives from the notion of the 'woven thing'.

4. A 'type', or 'typological reading', derives from a central idea of ancient textual interpretation (still important today) – that certain texts or stories were written, or were meant to be understood, in the light of other stories. These archetypal stories were like the master-dies from which coins were struck, that is the types that imprinted and characterised the other stories. Christian approaches to the Old Testament extensively read the older books as being types of the Christ events. On top of typological understandings the Christians superimposed the sense that the types were less the archetypes of the later Christ events, and really only their shadowy foretelling. Thus in a paradoxical sense the type became dependent on the later story for its authoritative interpretation within Christian textual approaches. A typical example of a typological reading is given in the Old Testament narrative of Isaac's sacrifice. As he carries the wood for the sacrifice up the hill, not knowing that he is himself the intended sacrificial victim – this was extensively read in patristic exegesis as a typological reference to Jesus' death, where he too carried the wood (the cross) to his own mountain of sacrifice: thus the correlated reading of the two stories shows Jesus as the new Isaac, and demonstrates how the death of the Lord fulfils all the aspirations of the Old Testament for the restoration of communion with God. This pattern of reading stories within stories is not as systematically applied in modern literary analysis as it was in late antiquity, but has once again become an important aspect of hermeneutical theory in contemporary times.

5. cf. J.A. McGuckin, *St Gregory of Nazianzus: An Intellectual Biography* (New York, 2000); idem, *St Gregory Nazianzen. Selected Poems* (Oxford, 1986, 1989, 1995); C. Moreschini and D. Sykes, *St Gregory of Nazianzus: Poemata Arcan* (Oxford, 1997); C. White, *Gregory of Nazianzus. Autobiographical Poems* (Cambridge, 1996).

6. *Theological Hymns* 1.1.34.

7. Text and translation in C. Trypanis, *The Penguin Book of Greek Verse* (London, 1971), pp. 374–89.

8. *Romanos. Kontakion 1. On the Nativity.*

9. *Romanos. The Lament of the Virgin. Kontakion 19.*

10. *Kontakion 22. On The Victory of the Cross.*

11. Greek text in Trypanis, *The Penguin Book of Greek Verse*, p. 435.

12. cf. McGuckin, *At the Lighting of the Lamps*, pp. 76–7.

13. *ibid.*, pp. 78–9.

CHAPTER 6. SAINTS AND THEIR HAGIOGRAPHIES IN BYZANTIUM

1. E. Miller, *Manuelis Philae Carmina* (vol. 1, Paris, 1855), p. 387.

2. *The Sayings of the Fathers, c. 56.*

3. Besa, *Life of Shenoute, c. 79*, tr. D.N. Bell (Kalamazoo, 1983).
4. *Sayings of the Desert Fathers. Alphabetical Collection. Iota. 7.*
5. A. Papadopoulos-Kerameus, *Sylloge palaistines kai syriakes hagiologias* (vol. 1, St Petersburg, 1907), p. 214.
6. D.Z. Sophianos, *Hosios Loukas. Ho Bios tou Hosiou Loukas tou Steriote* (Athens, 1989), p. 165.
7. Besa, *Life of Shenoute*, pp. 18–19, 58.
8. *Life of Mary the Younger, c. 3.*

CHAPTER 7. THE LUMINOUS SILENCE OF HESYCHASM

1. cf. J.A. McGuckin, 'St Symeon the New Theologian and Byzantine Monasticism', in A. Bryer (ed.), *Mount Athos and Byzantine Monasticism* (London, 1996), pp. 17–35. For a wider-ranging Life of Symeon: cf. B. Krivicheine, *In the Light of Christ* (New York, 1986).
2. cf. J.A. McGuckin. 'The Notion of Luminous Vision in 11th Century Byzantium: Interpreting the Biblical and Theological Paradigms of St Symeon the New Theologian', in M. Mullett (ed.), *Work and Worship at the Theotokos Evergetis* (Belfast, 1997), pp. 99–123.
3. The greatest of the royal monasteries of the capital city. Its rule or Typikon, had already become standard as the archetype of most foundations of monastic rules in the later Byzantine world. It was led in various times by some of the great monastic leaders of the eastern empire, and was a centre of learning and manuscript copying and production.
4. *Hymns of Divine Love* 21. For a full collection of the Hymns in English see G. Maloney, *St Symeon the New Theologian: Hymns of Divine Love* (Denville, NJ, 1975, 1999); for an historical consideration cf. J.A. McGuckin, 'St Symeon the New Theologian: Byzantine Theological Renewal in Search of a Precedent' in *Studies in Church History* (vol. 33, Suffolk/New York, 1997), pp. 75–90.
5. *Hymns of Divine Love* 25.
6. *ibid.* 25.
7. *ibid.* 24.
8. *ibid.* 27.
9. *ibid.* 2.
10. *On Stillness and Prayer: 137 Texts* (PG. 150. 1240–1300); Additional Chapters (PG. 150. 1300–1304); *On The Signs of Grace and Delusion: For the Confessor Longinos* (PG. 150. 1304–1312); *On Stillness and The Two Methods of Prayer* (PG. 150. 1313–1329); *On Prayer: How the Hesychast ought to compose himself* (PG. 150. 1329–1345).
11. English translation in E. Kadloubovsky and G.E.H. Palmer, *Writings From the Philokalia on Prayer of the Heart* (London, 1951).
12. *Discourse on Prayer 2.*
13. *On Commandments & Doctrines* 1.112.
14. Hebrews 8:1–2.

15. *On Commandments and Doctrines* 1.43.
16. *ibid.* 1.12.
17. *ibid.* 1.42.
18. *ibid.* 11.58–9.
19. *ibid.* 1.113.
20. *ibid.* 1.116.
21. So called as it was a collection of three volumes each in three groups.
22. *Triad.* 3.
23. *One Hundred and Fifty Texts* 93.
24. *ibid.* 72–3.
25. *Triads* 1.193.4.
26. Colossians 2:9.
27. Mark 9:1–7; cf. J.A. McGuckin. *The Transfiguration of Christ in Scripture and Tradition* (New York, 1987).
28. *Triads* 1.3.38.
29. *One Hundred and Fifty Texts* 65, 78.
30. *ibid.* 75.
31. *ibid.* 146–7.
32. *Triads* 1.3.21.

CHAPTER 8. 'THOUGH THERE STAND AROUND YOU TENS OF THOUSANDS OF ANGELS'

1. The beginnings of the nation of Russia, when it was a federation of princes. The principality that had Kiev as its capital was the most important. When this became Christianised, under Byzantine influence, the resulting impact was very significant on the Slavic nations.
2. No musical instruments are allowed in Orthodox services – only the human voice considered as God's own, directly created, instrument.
3. The best modern edition is *The Divine Liturgy of Our Father Among the Saints John Chrysostom* (Oxford, 1995).
4. Known as *Ektenies*.
5. The word means 'lifting up' as in a sacred offering of the Prayer of Thanksgiving.
6. The structure of the Orthodox churches is also meant to evoke the plan of the Temple of God as described in the Old Testament: with an outer court (the porch or narthex), an inner court of the faithful (the nave), and the Holy of Holies (the altar area behind the iconostasis). The opening of the doors of the iconostasis during times of prayer, especially the divine liturgy, signifies the inrush of the Kingdom of God into this age.
7. The Trisagion Prayers include the Trisagion itself (Holy God, Holy Mighty, Holy Immortal, have mercy on us), but also include a range of other intercessions culminating in the Our Father.
8. The Orthodox always use the term 'Pascha' (the early Christian word)

in preference to the Saxon word 'Easter' which derives from the name of the pagan goddess of Spring Yeostre.

9. On Wednesdays and Fridays no meat or dairy products are consumed. Stricter fasts exclude fish, oil, and wine, and also reduce the number and extent of meals taken. Monasteries have three fast days in the course of a week. The laity, as a rule, fast less than the monks, except when they are preparing for a particular spiritual occasion, or seeking God's special help in some personal matter.

10. S. Bulgakov, *The Orthodox Church* (1935; repr. New York, 1988), p. 132.

11. cf. N.M. Vaporis (ed.), *Daily Prayers for Orthodox Christians* (Brookline, Ma., 1986), or *A Manual of Eastern Orthodox Prayers* (first published London, 1945, eleventh impression 1991, and also issued New York, 1983).

BIBLIOGRAPHY

GENERAL TEXTS

Connor, C.L. *Art and Miracles in Medieval Byzantium: The Crypt at Hosios Loukas and its Frescoes*, Princeton, 1991.

Cross, L. *Eastern Christianity: The Byzantine Tradition*, Fairfax, Virginia, 1999.

Geanakoplos, D.J. *Byzantium: Church, Society, and Civilisation Seen Through Contemporary Eyes* (A Reader), Chicago, 1984.

Hausherr, I. *The Name of Jesus*, Kalamazoo, 1978.

Jones, C., G. Wainwright and E. Yarnold (eds.). *The Study of Spirituality*, London & New York, 1986.

Kadloubovsky, E., and G. Palmer. *Writings from the Philokalia on Prayer of the Heart*, London, 1992.

Maguire, H. *The Icons of their Bodies: Saints and their Images in Byzantium*, Princeton, 1996.

McGinn, B., J. Meyendorff and J. Leclercq (eds.). *Christian Spirituality: Origins to the 12th C.*, New York, 1993.

Meyendorff, J., *Byzantine Theology*, New York, 1975.

Palmer, G., P. Sherrard, & K. Ware (eds.). *The Philokalia*, 5 vols., London, 1979.

Runciman, S. *Byzantine Style and Civilisation*, London, 1975, 1990.

Spidlik, T. *The Spirituality of the Christian East*, Kalamazoo, 1986.

Talbot, A.M. *Holy Women of Byzantium*, Ten Saints' Lives in English Translation, Dumbarton Oaks, 1996.

Waddell, H. *The Desert Fathers*, London, 1962.

Ware, T. (ed.). *The Art of Prayer: An Orthodox Anthology*, London, 1981.

INDIVIDUAL CHAPTERS

Chapter 2

Studies

Clément, O. *The Roots of Christian Mysticism*, New York, 1995.

Lossky, V. *The Mystical Theology of the Eastern Church*, London, 1957.

— *In the Image and Likeness of God*, New York, 1974.

Runciman, S. *Byzantine Style and Civilisation*, London, 1975.

Ware, T. *The Orthodox Church*, London, 1963, 1987.

— *The Orthodox Way*, London, 1979.

Chapter 3

Texts in English Translation

Bamberger, J.E. *Evagrius Ponticus: Praktikos and Chapters on Prayer*, Cistercian Studies Series no. 4, Kalamazoo, 1972, 1981.

Driscoll, J. 'The *Ad Monachos* of Evagrius Ponticus: Its structure and a select commentary' in *Studia Anselmiana* 104 (1991).

Palmer, G., P. Sherrard and K. Ware (eds.). *The Philokalia*, vol. 1, London, 1979 – chapters on Evagrios: On Asceticism, On Discrimination, and On Prayer, pp. 29–71.

Studies

Chitty, D. *The Desert a City*, Oxford, 1966, pp. 49–53.

Driscoll, J. 'A Key for reading the *Ad Monachos* of Evagrius Ponticus' in *Augustinianum* 30 (1990), 361–92.

Hausherr, I. *Les leçons d'un contemplatif*, Paris, 1960.

Lemaitre, J. and R. Roques. 'Evagre' in M. Villier (ed.), *Dictionnaire de Spiritualité* vol. 2, Paris, 1953, cols. 1775–85.

Louth, A. *The Origins of the Christian Mystical Tradition*, Oxford, 1981, pp. 100–13.

Chapter 4

Texts in English Translation

Maloney, G. (tr.). *Pseudo Makarios: The Fifty Spiritual Homilies and the Great Letter*, Classics of Western Spirituality, New York, 1992.

Moore, L. (tr.). *St John Climacus: The Ladder of Divine Ascent*, second edn, Boston, Mass., 1991.

Palmer, G., P. Sherrard and K. Ware (eds., trs.). *Philokalia*, vol. 1, London, 1979 – writings of Diadochus of Photike.

Rose, S. (tr.). *Saints Barsanuphius and John: Guidance Toward Spiritual Life. Answers to the Questions of Disciples*, Platina, California, 1990.

Wheeler, E.P. (ed., tr.). *Dorotheos of Gaza: Discourses and Saying*, Cistercian Studies No. 33, Kalamazoo, 1977.

Studies

Brock, S. 'The Prayer of the Heart in Syriac Tradition' in *Sobornost* 4.2 (1982), pp. 131–42.

— *The Syriac Fathers on Prayer and the Spiritual Life*, Kalamazoo, 1987.

Jones, C., G. Wainwright and E. Yarnold (eds.). *The Study of Spirituality*, London & New York, 1986 – esp. sections 4.1 & 4, and 6.1–3, on

Eastern Christian Spirituality by Kallistos Ware, pp. 159–60, 175–83, 235–58.

Maloney, G. *The Prayer of the Heart*, Indiana, 1981.

McGinn, B., J. Meyendorff and J. Leclercq (eds.). 'Ways of Prayer and Contemplation (Eastern)' in *Christian Spirituality: Origins to the 12th C.*, New York, 1993, pp. 395–414.

McGuckin, J.A. 'The Prayer of the Heart in Patristic and Early Byzantine Tradition' in *Prayer and Spirituality in the Early Church*, vol. 2, ed. P. Allen, W. Mayer, and L. Cross, Queensland, 1999, pp. 69–108.

Neyt, F. 'The Prayer of Jesus', *Sobornost* Series 6 no. 9 (1974), 641–54.

Spidlik, T. *The Spirituality of the Christian East*, Kalamazoo, 1986.

Ware, K. (ed.). *The Art of Prayer*, compiled by Igumen Chariton, tr. E. Kadloubovsky and E.M. Palmer, London, 1966, 1981.

Chapter 5

Texts in Translation

Carpenter, M. *Romanos the Melodist*, 2 vols., ET & Comm. Columbia, Ohio, 1970–3.

Lash, E. (tr.). *St Romanos The Melodist: Kontakia on the Life of Christ*, New York/London, 1996.

McGuckin, J.A. *At The Lighting of the Lamps*, Harrisburg, Pa., 1997.

Trypanis, C. *The Penguin Book of Greek Verse*, London, 1971, pp. 392–414.

Studies

Topping, E.C. 'St Romanos: Ikon of a Poet' in *Greek Orthodox Theological Review* 12, No. 1 (1966), 92–111.

— 'St Romanos the Melodos and his First Nativity Kontakion' in *Greek Orthodox Theological Review* 21 (1976), 231–50.

— 'St Romanos the Melodos: Prince of Byzantine Poets' in *Greek Orthodox Theological Review* 24 (1979), 65–75.

Chapter 6

Texts in Translation

Besa. *The Life of Shenoute*, tr. D.N. Bell, Kalamazoo, 1983.

Dawes, E. and N. Baynes. *Three Byzantine Saints*, Oxford, 1948.

Talbot, A.M. *Ten Byzantine Women Saints' Lives*, Washington, 1997.

— *Faith Healing in Late Byzantium*, Brookline, Mass., 1983.

Ward, B. *Harlots of the Desert*, Kalamazoo, 1987.

Studies

Hackel, S. (ed.). *The Byzantine Saint*, London, 1981.

Harrison, V. 'The Feminine Man in Late Antique Ascetic Piety' in *Union Seminary Quarterly Review* 48, 3–4 (1994), 49–71.

McNamara, J.A. 'Muffled Voices': The Lives of Consecrated Women in the

4th C' in J.A. Nichols and L.T. Shank (eds.), *Medieval Religious Women: Distant Echoes*, Kalamazoo, 1984, pp. 11–29.

Pantel, P.S. *From Ancient Goddesses to Christian Saints*, tr. A. Goldhammer, Cambridge, Mass., 1992; cf. ch. 9 by M. Alexandre.

Poe, G.R. 'The Spirituality of Fourth and Fifth Century Eastern Female Asceticism as Reflected in the Life of St. Syncletica', Dissertation, Southern Baptist Theological Seminary, 1995.

Chapter 7

Texts in Translation

de Catanzaro, C.J. *Symeon the New Theologian. The Discourses* (Catecheses), Classics of Western Spirituality, New York, 1980.

Gendle, N. (tr.). *St Gregory Palamas. The Triads*, Classics of Western Spirituality, New York, 1983.

Maloney, G. *Symeon the New Theologian. Hymns of Divine Love*, New Jersey, 1975, 1999.

McGuckin, P. (tr.). *St Symeon the New Theologian. Practical, Theological, and Gnostic Chapters*, Cistercian Studies, vol. 41, Kalamazoo, 1982.

Palmer, G., P. Sherrard and K. Ware (eds.). *The Philokalia*, vol. 4, London, 1995 – select works of St Symeon, St Gregory of Sinai, and St Gregory Palamas, pp. 212–86.

Sinkewicz, R. *St Gregory Palamas: The One Hundred and Fifty Chapters*, Pontifical Institute of Medieval Studies and Texts Series, vol. 83, Toronto, 1988.

Studies

Balfour, D. 'St Gregory of Sinai's Life Story and Spiritual Profile' in *Theologia* 53 (1982), 30–62.

— *St Gregory the Sinaite: Discourse on the Transfiguration*, offprint from *Theologia*, Athens, 1983.

Hausherr, I., *The Spirituality of the Christian East*, Kalamazoo, 1980.

— *The Name of Jesus*, Kalamazoo, 1978.

Jones, C., G. Wainwright and E. Yarnold (eds.). *The Study of Spirituality*, Oxford, 1986, esp. sections 4 and 6 by Kallistos Ware, pp. 235f.

Krivocheine, B. *In the Light of Christ. St Symeon the New Theologian*, New York, 1986.

McGinn, B. and J. Meyendorff. *Christian Spirituality*, vol. 1., Origins to 12th Century, New York, 1993 – ch. 16 by Kallistos Ware.

McGuckin, J.A. 'The Notion of Luminous Vision in 11th C. Byzantium: Interpreting the Biblical and Theological Paradigms of St Symeon the New Theologian' in *Work & Worship at the Theotokos Evergeti*, Acts of the Belfast Byzantine Colloquium, Portaferry, 1995, ed. M. Mullett, Belfast, 1997, pp. 90–123.

— 'St Symeon the New Theologian (d. 1022): Byzantine theological renewal in search of a precedent' in *Studies in Church History*, vol. 33 (The Church Retrospective), Suffolk/New York, 1997, pp. 75–90.

Meyendorff, J. *A Study of Gregory Palamas*, New York, 1964.

— *St Gregory Palamas and Orthodox Spirituality*, New York, 1974.

— *Byzantine Hesychasm*, London, 1974.

Turner, H.J.M. *St Symeon the New Theologian and Spiritual Fatherhood*, Leiden, 1990.

Ware, K. 'The Jesus Prayer in St Gregory of Sinai' in *Eastern Churches Review*, vol. 4 (1972), pp. 3–32.

Chapter 8

Studies

Bulgakov, S. *The Orthodox Church*, rev. edn, New York, 1988.

Hopko, T. *The Lenten Spring*, New York, 1983.

— *The Winter Pascha*, New York, 1984.

Jungmann, J. *Christian Prayer Through the Centuries*, New York, 1978.

Mazza, E. *Mystagogy: A Theology of Liturgy in the Patristic Age*, New York, 1989.

Ware, T. *The Orthodox Church*, London, 1963.

Wybrew, H. *The Orthodox Liturgy*, London, 1989.

SHORT GLOSSARY

Aisthesis – sensibility.
In Byzantine thought in the early Syrian tradition it was used to connote the manner in which a Christian could psychically experience the activities of the Holy Spirit within the workings of the soul and body. Early writers insisted that the spiritual life had to be 'conscious', and that without the sensed experience of the Spirit of God, the soul was languishing. Later Byzantine thinkers in the tenth century (and after in the medieval Hesychast movement) adapted the idea to argue for the necessity of personal experience in the advancing stages of the spiritual life to counteract religious formalism. Spiritual 'experience' was always afforded a high status in the Byzantine tradition, and someone who had not 'experienced' the spiritual mysteries was heavily discouraged from pretending to advise anyone else in matters of spirituality.

Anabasis – ascension.
In the New Testament (especially the Fourth Gospel) it is the word used to describe the ascending of the Logos of God to divine glory. In Byzantine writing it connotes the manner in which the soul has an instinct to rise up to transcendent mysteries, and seek after divine things. The soul was seen as naturally ascentive, and in the rising to spiritual closeness with God the Byzantines felt the human spirit became true to itself, true to its purpose in being, true that is to the pattern of its original creation by God.

Apatheia – dispassion.
The Byzantine understanding of the human person considered the 'passions' as forces external to the self that could, if they were not checked and disciplined, emerge as uncontrollable obsessions that enslaved the psyche. If disciplined and set in right order, the passions could be used as major avenues of training in virtue. So the passion of acquisitiveness, for example, could serve as a major stimulus for a person to work honourably and creatively to support a family, and also to offer almsgiving to the poor, but if disordered could lead to deep selfishness and social inequity. At a stage when all the virtues had been practised so assiduously that they had become a deep-rooted habit of the soul, the Byzantines thought that

an advanced disciple was unlikely to be tempted by the things that once could seduce them (in the way, perhaps, a vegetarian of many years' standing no longer experiences the smell of cooking meat as even vaguely attractive). In such a disciple, they thought, a state of psychic dis-passion had been reached. It was a state of elevated spiritual calm and concentration that allowed the higher mystical states to occur within the psyche, states that were normally hindered by the amount of psychic 'noise' and distraction involved in the day-to-day disciplining of the unruly passions in most people. Monks who had achieved the dispassionate state were expected to serve as spiritual elders (*Staretsi*) to other seekers.

Hegemonikon – the ruling principle of the self.

The self, in Byzantine thought, was a composite reality, a joining together of several disparate elements, into a collection. Spirit and flesh were parts of that collation, but the totality was much more complex and involved the manner in which all the various passions related together – as either a cacophony of warring needs, or as a symphonic harmony. The term was used in Byzantine spiritual writing to connote the way in which the spiritual self establishes a hierarchy of values and orientations. The *hegemonikon* itself was often considered to be the soul's intellective vision (the *nous* or the logos of a person) in which respect it was considered to be the image of the Image of God (or an individual logos-soul created in the image of the Divine Logos). If the individual person allowed their logos-instinct to be the dominant aspect of all they strove for, and ultimately all they were, the Byzantine teachers taught that spiritual harmony and progress would inevitably follow.

Hesychia – stillness.

In early Byzantine literature it is a synonym for the state of the monk, a person, male or female, who seeks a life of quiet withdrawal to devote himself or herself to prayer (becoming a hesychast). In later medieval Byzantine thought it came to refer particularly to a school of spirituality (Hesychasm) that taught the need to quieten the spiritual senses by the regular and slow repetition of short prayers (especially the Jesus Prayer) so that the one who prayed could become focused and attentive to the workings of God's Spirit in the heart.

Kalokagathon – the good and the true.

Pre-Christian Greek philosophic and moral thought related the two ideas together as an image of the ideal state of religion and ethics. Christianity added to the old philosophic ideas the stress, closely related to the doctrine of the incarnation, that the good and the true would (ultimately) be synonymous with the beautiful, and all would be harmonised in the soul's experience of union with the Logos.

Katabasis – descent; the paired term in the Fourth Gospel, with *anabasis*.

The action of the Logos was seen in Byzantine thought to be typified by the Evangelist's teaching that the Divine Word has descended to earth for the salvation of the race, and would ascend once more in glory, taking souls with him. Individuals who ascended to God, did so only on the basis of God's compassionate *katabasis* to them in advance. The Byzantine spiritual teaching on God's *katabasis* in compassion is comparable to the western Church's teaching on prevenient grace, though less formally constructed than the latter.

Kenosis – self emptying-out.

It is the term Paul uses in Philippians 2:6–11 to describe the *katabasis* of God in the incarnation. For the Byzantines the incarnation becomes the archetypal symbol and actual method of the outreach of God to his creatures.

Logismos (logismoi) – thoughts, ideations.

In the teaching of the desert monks (especially Evagrios), the state of spiritual calmness (*hesychia*) is constantly disrupted by teeming thoughts that often arise, unbidden, in a person's psyche. Advancing into pure prayer could only be done when mental imagery and ideas had been radically stilled. The *logismoi* are always regarded as a major hindrance to the state of prayer, which in its refined state is regarded as transcending thoughts, images, and dialogues.

Nous – the spiritual intellect.

The Byzantines regarded the *nous* as the main spiritual and psychic individuality of a person. It corresponds to what much later, western, writing refers to as 'the soul'. The soul (psyche) in eastern Christian literature mainly referred to the powers of sensibility a person had (feelings of love or grief or suchlike) whereas the *nous* connoted the faculty a person had for spiritual understanding. It was related to, but quite distinct from, the mind or rational power of a human being (the individual *logos*), and always referred to the capacity of an intelligent creature for the transcendent encounter with God, in prayer.

Parousia – literally, the Presence.

It became a technical word in the New Testament for the 'Second Coming' of Christ, when he would return at the end of time to inaugurate the Last Judgement.

Theosis – deification.

In the later writings of the New Testament and in most Greek patristic theological writing, it is the principle of God's salvific action in the world. It refers to the way in which God stoops down to history in the incarnation (*katabasis*) in order to lift up his creatures to transcendent union with God (*anabasis*). Athanasios of Alexandria expressed the idea classically by saying: 'The Word became Man that we might become god.' For the Byzantines, to become god, or become divinised, meant to arrive at such an association with God's presence that the person entered into communion with God by grace. The phrase is deliberately used by Byzantine spiritual writers because it is so stark and shocking in its connotations. It always has to be understood correctly by means of two constant presuppositions: (a) that the gift of divine communion is initiated at God's invitation, and (b) that it is a deification by grace that immortalises the soul because of its nearness to the Lord who is the source of its life. These two ideas radically separate off the Byzantine notion of deification from pagan uses of the term, and also show it to be a notion corresponding to the western term 'grace', though a far more dynamically conceived system of redemption.